All the Types and Shadows of the Old Testament

with commentary

DANIEL H. COE, SR. PH.D.

Charleston, AR
Cobb Publishing
2025

All the Types and Shadows of the Old Testament with Commentary is copyright © 2025 by Daniel H. Coe, Sr. All rights reserved.

No portion of this book may be reproduced in any form, whether print, digital, audio, video, or any other format without the prior written permission of the author and/or publisher.

Scripture quotations are from the King James Version.

Edited by Bradley S. Cobb

Published in the United States of America by:
Cobb Publishing
CobbPublishing.com
Editor@CobbPublishing.com
479.747.8372
See our website for more books about the Bible.

ISBN: 978-1-960858-41-2

Contents

Introduction v
The Creation: A Type of the Church 1
Adam: A Type of Christ 5
Eve: A Type of the Church 11
Abel: A Type of Christ 13
Seth: A Type of Christ 15
Enoch: A Type of Christ 17
The Ark: A Type of the Church 19
Noah: A Type of Christ 23
The Flood: A Type of Baptism 27
Job: A Type of Christ 29
Abraham: A Type of Christ 33
Melchizedek: A Type of Christ 39
Isaac: A Type of Christ 45
The Sons of Hagar and Sarah:
Allegorical Types of the Old Law and the New Law .. 49
Joseph: A Type of Christ 53
The Burning Bush: A Type of the Church 57
Moses: A Type of Christ 59
The Tabernacle:
A Type of the New Testament Church 63
Egypt:
A Type of Bondage in Sin and Spiritual Death 77

Israelite Homes During the Death of the Firstborn:
A Type of the Church 81

Pharaoh: A Type of Satan 93

The Passover Lamb: A Type of Christ....................... 97

Crossing the Red Sea: A Type of Baptism 101

Manna from Heaven: A Type of Christ 109

The Smitten Rock: A Type of Christ 113

Mount Sinai: A Type of Mount Zion 117

Moses' Transfiguration:
A Type of Christ's Transfiguration 121

The Intercession of Moses for the People:
A Type of Christ Interceding for the Saints............. 127

The Consecration of Aaron:
A Type of the Consecration of Christ...................... 133

The Levites: A Type of Christians............................ 137

The Brazen Serpent: A Type of Christ.................... 143

The Cities of Refuge: Types of the Church 149

The Two Goats: A Type of Christ 161

Leprosy: A Type of Sin 167

The Sabbatical Year and the Year of Jubilee:
Types of the Gospel Age 175

Joshua: A Type of Christ.. 183

Rahab: A Type of the Redeemed Church............... 185

The Judges: Types of Christ 193

Ruth: A Type of the Redeemed Church.................. 197

Boaz: A Type of Christ 199

Samuel: A Type of Christ 203

David: A Type of Christ 209
Ahithophel: A Type of Judas Iscariot 213
Solomon: A Type of Christ 215
Elijah: A Type of John The Baptizer 219
Elisha: A Type of Christ 227
Hezakiah: A Type of Christ 233
Ezra: A Type of Christ 237
Nehemiah: A Type of Christ 247
Zerubbabel: A Type of Christ 251
Types From The Book Of Esther 255
Esther: A Type of Christ and the Church 257
Mordecai: A Type of Christ 259
Haman: A Type of Satan 261
The Jews: A Type of the Victorious Church 263
Hosea: A Type of Christ 265
Jonah: A Type of Christ. 269

Introduction

The Old Testament paints clear pictures of most everything in the New Testament. It, therefore, does one well to look for the pictures in God's book regarding the scheme of redemption and see just how accurately God painted pictures of Christ, the church, the apostles, and other men, women, and other subjects. No book but the Bible has ever been so perfectly composed, providing such portraits of God's will.

Our Father was first to take in hand the golden needle of prophecy, into the eye of which He placed the scarlet thread of the scheme of redemption, so dyed by the blood of Christ. He then began to stitch into the tapestry of time, scenes of His Divine plan. God then passed that golden needle of prophecy to each of His inspired prophets, who, in turn, stitched additional beauties of Christ and the church into that tapestry, fully revealing God's eternal plan *"according to the eternal purpose which he purposed in Christ Jesus our Lord"* (Eph. 3:11).

The tapestry of God's handiwork, which featured His Son on the cross and the establishment of the church on the day of Pentecost, came to fruition and into full view. A beautiful picture indeed. Bible students do well to look for Jesus and the church in every passage of the inspired text. Care must exercised, however, not to overly spiritualize.

Spiritualizing is the act of making something spiritual; strongly infusing it with spiritual or allegorizing content. Denominationalists have long tethered themselves to

All the Types and Shadows of the Old Testament

spiritualizing many things which are not in the least warranted. For example, one may spiritualize the three levels of Noah's ark as representing the Father, Son, and Holy Spirit. Indeed, such is a far stretch of the imagination. On the other hand; some insist there are no fitting reasons to spiritualize anything. Both approaches are wrong and must be properly balanced when considering ante-types and anti-types of the Old Testament. An ante-type is a *before* type of an individual, place or event, an anti-type is type *in contrast to* an individual, place or event.

Most important in the study of types and shadows of the Old Testament is to read every passage pertaining to the type under consideration:

> *For the law having a shadow of good things to come, and not the very image of the things, can never with those sacrifices which they offered year by year continually make the comers thereunto perfect (Heb. 10:1).*

Paul wrote, concerning the matter of types and shadows:

> *"For whatsoever things were written aforetime were written for our learning, that we through patience and comfort of the scriptures might have hope" (Rom. 15:4).*

Again, Paul declared:

> *"Now all these things happened unto them for ensamples: and they are written for our admonition, upon whom the ends of the world are come" (I Cor. 10:11).*

The author of Hebrews wrote:

> *"It was therefore necessary that the patterns of things in the heavens should be purified with*

Introduction

these; but the heavenly things themselves with better sacrifices than these" (Heb. 9:23).

In the passages cited heretofore, five inspired remarks should capture the attention of the student of God's Word. First, one should notice the phrase *types and shadows*. Inspiration made it absolutely clear the Old Testament contains such and warrants the close eye of the student. Secondly, Paul wrote: *whatsoever things were written aforetime were written for our learning.* Countless is the number of brethren in the Lord's church who foolishly insist the study of the Old Testament is superfluous and is of little use and does not benefit the church. Third, inspiration informs us *"all these things happened unto them for ensamples."* When the Scripture declares a matter serves as example, it needs the diligent eye of study. Further, we are plainly told such things are *"written for our admonition."* Admonition comes in numerous forms, and many things of the Old Testament prove to be the case.

Both the Patriarchal and the Mosaic dispensations have types and shadows of Christ, the church, and other New Testament subjects recorded. When one properly studies the types and shadows of the Old Testament, his New Testament becomes much more alive and meaningful. The wisdom of the Father is beyond compare, but He has provided for us a clear picture of Christ, the church, baptism, the apostles, and even John the baptizer along with many other New Testament figures and matters.

All the Types and Shadows of the Old Testament

The Creation: A Type of the Church

Few consider the creation serves as a picture of the Lord's church in type. Yet there is seen in that event a clear display of the church.

Numerous adumbrative portraits have been painted on the pages of Inspiration for the Bible student who looks intently at the Word of God. Suggestion is here made and strongly encouraged for the Bible student to observe the many pictures the Divine hand of the God provided in the miraculous events of creation. It is well for every Bible student to look for Jesus, the church and other New Testament matters in every passage of inspired script. As the Lord and His church are prefigured in the Old Testament, so it is the case the apostles, John the baptizer and others and other events are also prefigured therein by way of types. As noted in the Introduction of this effort: The Old Testament is The New Testament concealed, and the New Testament is the Old Testament revealed. Therefore, it does the Bible student well to open the pages of Holy writ and look for the many things concealed in the Old Testament which come into clear view in the New Testament. Doing so makes one's Bible come very much alive and assures honest Bible students the Bible is indeed the inspired word of God.

All the Types and Shadows of the Old Testament

1. In the beginning of creation everything about came by miracle (Gen. 1–2).

- God made the earth and the heavenly bodies from nothing.
- God made every living thing from nothing, except Adam and Eve.
- Out of the dust of the earth God made man.

The beginning of the church came by miracle on Pentecost (Acts 2:1–4).

- The apostles were Divinely guided into all truth when the church began.
- The apostles spoke in differing languages (tongues).

2. The garden of Eden was a perfectly prepared place (Gen. 1:10; 2:8-15. God saw *it was good*).

The church is a perfectly prepared place (Heb. 11:10; I Pet. 2:5).

The Creation: A Type of the Church

3. Creation had perfectly prepared people (Gen. 1:26. Made in *the image of God*).

Those in the church are His perfect workmanship (Eph. 2:10. The Lord's church is perfect, made up of imperfect people made perfect by the blood of Christ).

4. The garden of Eden required care and tending, Adam was to dress and keep it (Gen. 2:15).

The church needs care and tending, and must be fed by her caretakers (Acts 20:28; I Tim. 3:15; I Pet. 5:2-3).

5. Creation had a perpetual source of water, for there was a mist which went up from the ground and watered the earth (Gen. 2:6).

The church has a perpetual source of *living* water in Christ (John 4:10–14).

6. At creation, a perpetual source of food was provided for the first inhabitants of the earth. God provided them *every tree* (Gen. 2:16).

In the church there is a perpetual source of food. Christ is *the bread of life* (John 6:48).

7. Everything in creation was made fully mature, already producing seed after its kind (Gen 1:21, 31).

In the church the apostle were fully *guided into all truth*, and ready to produce fruit (John 16:13).

8. All God created produced after its kind, it's seed was in itself (Gen. 1:11).

In the church *the seed is the word of God*, and produces *after its* kind (Luke 8:11; I Pet. 1:23; Jas. 1:18).

All the Types and Shadows of the Old Testament

9. At creation God provided a great light: *Let there be light (*Gen. 1:3*).*

The church has a great light in Christ; He said plainly: *I am the light of the world (*John 8:12*).*

10. Creation had Divinely created inhabitants. God made man (Gen. 1:26).

God makes saints new creatures in the church (II Cor. 5:17).

11. The creation had a great light and lesser lights (Gen. 1:16–17).

The church has a great light and lesser lights (John 8:12; Eph. 5:8).

12. God removed Adam from the garden because of disobedience (Gen. 3:23).

Disobedient saints will be removed from the church by the Lord (Matt. 7:23; 25:30; I Cor. 5:13; 2 Thes. 3:6).

13. Man was added to the garden by the Lord (Gen. 1:26).

Obedient men are added to the church by the Lord (Acts 2:47; 5:14).

Adam: A Type of Christ

The account of Adam and his having been made by God from the dust of the earth is simple and has been rehearsed by countless Bible-school teachers for centuries. Yet very little attention has been awarded to Adam so far as the events of his life and creation are portraits of Christ.

That the church would be better served by observing the pictures concealed in the events of Adam's creation and life is true and needs frequent teaching. Observe that which the apostle Paul wrote regarding Adam and Christ. Paul identifies the first man—Adam—as the *first Adam*. Christ is identified by the apostle as the *second Adam*. Because inspiration identified Christ as the *second Adam*, such forever settles the matter the *first Adam* being a type of Christ.

> *And so it is written, The first man Adam was made a living soul; the second Adam was made a quickening spirit (I Cor. 15:45).*

1. The first Adam *turned away from* the Father in the garden of Eden (Gen. 3:1–10).

The second Adam *turned to* the Father in the garden of Gethsemane (Matt. 26:36, 39; Phil. 2:8).

2. The first Adam was naked and unashamed (Gen. 2:25).

The second Adam was naked and bore shame on the cross (Matt. 27:28; Heb. 12:2).

All the Types and Shadows of the Old Testament

3. The first Adam was named by the Father (Gen. 5:2).
The second Adam was named by the Father (Luke 1:31).

4. The first Adam had no earthy father (Gen. 2:7).
The second Adam has no earthly father (Luke 1:34-35; Matt. 1:18-23).

5. The first Adam's sin brought about thorns (Gen. 3:17-18; Rom. 5:12).
The second Adam wore a crown of thorns because of sin (John 19:2).

6. The first Adam gave his name to his bride (Gen. 3:20).
The second Adam gave the name to His bride (Isa. 62:2; Acts 11:26).

7. The first Adam substituted himself for God (Gen. 3:5).
The second Adam was God substituting Himself for man (Rom. 8:3; II Cor. 5:21; I Pet. 3:18).

8. The first Adam sinned at a tree (Gen. 2:17; 3:6).
The second Adam became sin on a tree (Gal. 3:13).

9. The first Adam died *because of sin* (Gen. 2:17; 3:3).
The second Adam *died for sin (*Matt. 26:28; Heb. 9:28*)*.

10. The first Adam lost access to the tree of life (Gen. 3:22).
The second Adam provides saints access to the tree of life, Rev, 22:14.

Adam: A Type of Christ

11. The first Adam was the head of the physical creation (Gen. 1:26–28).

The second Adam is the head of the spiritual creation (Dan. 7:13-14; I Pet. 3:22).

12. The first Adam was created in God's image (Gen. 1:27).

The second Adam is God's image (John 6:46; 14:9; Col. 1:15; II Cor. 4:4).

13. The first Adam was to reign over all the earth till the end life; Gen. 1:26–28.

The second Adam will reign over all the earth until the end of all time (I Cor 15:25–28).

14. The first Adam was the first husband (Gen. 3:6).

The second Adam is the saints' last husband (II Cor. 11:2; Eph. 5:30–32).

15. The first Adam was alone and needed an help meet (Gen. 2:18).

The second Adam was alone and needed a bride (Eph. 5:25–27, 31-32).

16. The first Adam was *given a wife (*Gen. 2:22*).*

The second Adam *purchased His wife (*Acts 20:28*).*

17. The first Adam was put into a deep physical sleep to produce his bride, Eve (Gen. 2:21).

The second Adam went in to the sleep of death to death to produce His bride, the church (Mark 8:31).

All the Types and Shadows of the Old Testament

18. The first Adam came out from the ground and returned to it (Gen. 3:19).

The second Adam went into the ground and came out of it (Matt. 28:6).

19. The first Adam became a living soul (Gen. 2:7

The second Adam is a quickening spirit (I Cor. 15:45

20. The first Adam died and returned to the ground, Gen. 3:19).

The second Adam died and returned to heaven (Acts 1:9–11).

21. The first Adam's side was opened to obtain his bride, Gen. 2:21).

The second Adam's side was pierced to purchase His bride (John 19:34; I Cor. 6:20; Acts 20:28).

22. Eve was made from the first Adam (Gen. 2:22).

The church was built by the second Adam (Matt. 16:18).

23. Eve was made with the first Adam's rib (Gen. 2:22).

The church was built with the second Adam's blood (I Pet. 1:18-19).

24. Eve was brought to the first Adam without sin (Gen. 2:22).

The church will be presented to the second Adam without sin (Eph. 5:27).

25. Eve was the same as the first Adam in life, nature and expression (Gen. 2:23).

The church is the same as the second Adam in life, nature and expression (Eph. 5:2, 27).

Adam: A Type of Christ

26. The first Adam and his bride became one flesh (Matt. 19:1–6).
The second Adam and the church are one in one spirit (Jno 17:20–22; I Cor. 12:13).

27. The first Adam was called the son of God (Luke 3:38).
The second Adam called the Son of God (John 3:16).

28. The first Adam was given power and dominion over creation (Gen. 1:26-28).
The second Adam was given power and dominion over all creation (Dan. 7:13-14; Matt. 28:18; Col 1:15-20).

29. The first Adam had but one bride (Gen. 5:1-2).
The second Adam has one bride (Rev. 21:2).

30. The first Adam came by miracle (Gen. 1:26).
The second Adam came by miracle (Isa. 7:14; Matt. 1:18).

31. The first Adam was created and died a physically old man (Gen. 5:5).
The second Adam died and creates spiritually new men (II Cor. 5:17).

32. The first Adam was the captain of damnation (Rom. 5:12–21).
The second Adam is the captain of salvation (Heb. 2:10).

33. The first Adam hid himself from God (Gen. 3:10).
The second Adam presents man to God (Eph. 5:27).

All the Types and Shadows of the Old Testament

34. The first Adam was clothed by God (Gen. 3:21).
The second Adam will clothe saints for God (Rev. 7:9).

35. The bride of the first Adam wore his name (Gen. 5:2).
The bride of the second Adam wears His name (Isa. 62:2; Acts 11:26).

36. The first Adam's disobedience brought death (Rom. 5:12).
The second Adam's obedience brings life (Rom. 5:17-19).

Eve:
A Type of the Church

In Eve there is clear picture of the Lord's church. Eve was God's first gift to man. Every woman/wife needs to understand she is to be an help meet (fitting) to and for her husband. Because woman is God's gift to man, every woman needs to conduct herself as such and be to and for her husband what God intends. Likewise, the husband must realize he is to treat his wife in the way God intends. The husband must treat his wife as a gift from God, for that she is. No wife has any problem submitting to a husband who treats her with the dignity and respect God mandated. No husband suffers ill from his wife when he treats her according the dictates of the Lord. The church has a perfect husband in Christ, therefore, the church is to be perfect in conduct and behavior as mandated by the Lord.

1. Eve was taken from Adam's side (Gen. 2:21).

Christ's side was opened to purchase the church (John 19:34-35; I John 5:6; Acts 20:28).

2. Eve was bone of Adam's bone and flesh of his flesh (Gen. 2:23).

The Church is the body of Christ (Eph. 5:30).

3. Eve was presented by God to Adam (Gen. 2:22).

The Church will be presented to Christ as His Bride (Eph. 5:27; Rev. 21:2; II Cor. 11:2).

All the Types and Shadows of the Old Testament

4. Eve was presented to Adam spotless and without sin (Gen. 2:22).
The Church is to be spotless and without blemish (Eph. 5:27).

5. Eve came about by miracle (Gen. 2:22).
The church came about by miracle (Acts 2:1–4).

6. Eve produced children, Cain, Abel, Seth (Gen. 4:1-2, 25).
The church is to produce children of God (Gal. 3:26-27; 4:26-27).

7. Eve was subject to her husband (Gen. 2:18; 3:16).
The church is subject to Christ (Eph. 1:22; 5:24; Col. 1:18.).

8. Eve was a helper to her husband (Gen. 2:18).
The church is to help Christ (I Cor. 15:58; II Cor. 6:1).

9. Eve was dressed by God (Gen. 3:21).
The church dressed by Christ (Rev. 6:11; Gal 3:27; Rev. 19:8).

10. Eve is the mother of all living (Gen. 3:20).
The church is made up of all spiritually living (I Tim. 3:15; Gal 4:26).

11. Eve was deceived by the serpent (II Cor. 11:3).
The church must guard against being deceived (II Cor 11:2-4).

12. Eve was named by Adam (Gen. 3:20).
The church is named by Christ (Acts 11:26; Isa. 62:2).

Abel: A Type of Christ

That Abel serves as a type of Christ in wonderful splendor is clear (Heb. 12:24). Few consider Abel in such a manner, yet the Scriptures are pristine in clarity and focus. Numerous comparisons are prefigured in Abel regarding the Lord, it does one well to look for the Lord in the short record recorded regarding Abel.

1. Abel was a shepherd (Gen. 4:2).
Christ is a shepherd (John 10:11-14; I Pet. 5:4; Heb. 13:20).

2. Abel presented an acceptable offering to God (Gen. 4:4; Heb. 11:4).
Christ was presented as an acceptable offering to God (John 10:11; Isa. 53:10; Eph. 5:2; Heb. 9:14).

3. Abel was hated by his brother (Gen. 4:8).
Christ was hated by His brethren (John 15:25).

4. Abel was slain by his brother (Gen. 4:8).
Christ was slain by His brethren (Matt. 27:18; John 1:11; Acts 7:52).

5. Abel did not die a natural death (Gen. 4:8).
Christ did not die a natural death (Acts 2:23).

6. Abel suffered a violent death (Gen. 4:8).
Christ suffered a violent death (Acts 2:23).

All the Types and Shadows of the Old Testament

7. Abel's murdered was punished (Gen. 4:11-12).
Christ's murderers will be punished (Heb. 6:6; Rev. 1:7).

8. Abel presented the firstlings of his flock, a lamb, to God (Gen. 4:4).
Christ was the firstborn lamb offered to God (Rom. 8:29; Rev. 13:8; I Pet. 1:19-20).

9. Abel believed the word of the Lord and obeyed it (Heb. 11:4).
Christ is the word of God who must be believed and obeyed (John 1:1; John 8:24).

10. Abel's sacrifice was excellent (Heb. 11:4).
Christ was a most excellent sacrifice (Eph. 5:2).

11. Abel's offering had God's respect (Heb. 11:4).
Christ's offering of Himself was respected by God (Isa. 53:10).

12. Abel obtained a good witness from God (Heb. 11:4).
Christ obtained a good witness from God (I Cor. 15:1–8; I Pet. 2:4).

13. Abel was counted righteous by faith (Heb. 11:4).
Christ was righteous and is our righteousness (Matt. 3:15; I Cor. 1:30).

14. Abel's offering was accepted by God (Heb. 11:4).
Christ's offering was accepted by God (Luke 2:52).

15. Abel, being dead yet speaks (Heb. 11:4).
Christ yet speaks (Heb. 1:1-2; 12:24; Rev. 5:6).

Seth: A Type of Christ

That Seth is a type of Christ is almost always unseen or unconsidered by even the most astute Bible students, yet, Seth being a type of Christ is powerfully clear. Seth, was the replacement seed child for Christ as declared by Eve in Genesis 4:25 (see also 3:15). Even though only a few verses are given space in the inspired record regarding Seth, there is much to gain in the Study of him

1. Seth appointed by God (Gen. 4:25).
Christ appointed by God (Heb. 1:2; Acts 2:36; I Pet. 2:4).

2. Seth was the seed of woman (Gen. 4:25).
Christ is the seed of woman (Gal. 4:4; Isa. 7:14).

3. Seth was given instead, or in behalf of, Abel (Gen. 4:25).
Christ was given in our stead on the cross (Heb. 9:28; I Pet. 3:18).

4. Through Seth men called upon God (Gen. 4:26).
Through Christ men call upon God (Acts 22:16; John 14:6).

5. Seth had many children (Gen. 5:7).
Christ has many children (Gal. 3:26).

All the Types and Shadows of the Old Testament

6. Seth was a man of God (Gen. 4:25).
Christ was a man of God (John 3:16).

7. Seth made after father's likeness (Gen. 5:3).
Christ made in His Father's likeness (John 14:9; Col. 1:15).

8. Seth named by his father (Gen. 4:25).
Christ named by the Father (Matt. 1:23).

9. Seth preserved the godly lineage (Gen. 5:4-32).
Christ preserves His people (John 17:12; Jude 25

Enoch:
A Type of Christ

Enoch further serves as a type of Christ. Of Enoch it is twice stated by Inspiration *he walked with God*, first in Gen. 5:22 and second in 5:24. Enoch was taken by the Lord because he walked with the Lord. All who follow the example of Enoch's walk are chosen and taken by the Lord).

Those who walk after the flesh and sow thereunto "*shall of the flesh reap corruption; but he that soweth to the Spirit shall of the Spirit reap life everlasting*" (Gal. 6:8). Enoch was a man in whom (similar to Christ) the Father was well pleased (Matt. 3:17).

1. Enoch was a man of great faith (Gen. 5:23-24).
Jesus was a man of great faith (Heb. 12:2; John 5:19-20).

2. Enoch was obedient to God (Gen. 5:22–24).
Jesus was obedient to God (Heb. 5:8; Phil. 2:8; John 8:29).

3. Enoch was *a son* of man (Gen. 5:18).
Jesus was *the son* of man (Matt. 8:20).

4. Enoch walked with God (Gen. 5:22).
Jesus walked with God (I John 2:6).

5. Enoch ascended to heaven (Gen. 5:24
Jesus ascended to heaven, Acts 1:11).

All the Types and Shadows of the Old Testament

6. Enoch pleased God well (Heb. 11:5).
Jesus pleased God well (Matt. 17:5).

7. Enoch was a prophet of God (Jude vs.14).
Jesus was a prophet of God, Matthew–John

8. Enoch prophesied of the judgment (Jude vs.15).
Jesus prophesied of the judgment (Matt. 25:31–46).

9. Enoch was awarded God's testimony (Heb. 11:5).
Jesus was awarded God's testimony (Matt. 17:5).

10. Enoch did not see death (Heb. 11:5).
Jesus tasted of death for every man (Heb. 2:9; John 10:17-18; Phil. 2:8).

11. Enoch was not found among the living (Heb. 11:5).
Jesus was not found among the dead (John 20:2; Luke 24:5-6; Acts 2:24).

12. Enoch begat sons and daughters (Gen. 5:22).
Jesus begets sons and daughters (I John 5:18; John 1:12-13; Heb. 2:10; Isa. 53:10).

13. Enoch received the testimony that he was pleasing to God (Heb. 11:4-6).
Jesus was vindicated as pleasing to God by His resurrection and ascension.

The Ark: A Type of the Church

The account of Noah and the ark has been one of the most told of the Bible. Sunday school teachers have taught young children the event for centuries. The number of sermons presented from Noah and the ark are known only to the Lord. Yet a picture of the ark Noah built has been placed upon the wall of time for Bible students to consider in a most in-depth way. Over a dozen comparisons between the ark, Christ and the church are provided on the pages of inspiration for consideration.

1. The Ark had one Master Builder, Noah (Gen. 6:14–16).
The Church has one Master Builder, Jesus (Matt. 16:18; Eph. 2:20-22; Heb. 3:3-4).

2. The Ark had one blueprint, one standard (Gen 6:14–16).
The Church has one blueprint, one standard (I Cor. 3:11; Eph. 3:10-11).

3. The Ark was made from one material, Gopher Wood (Gen. 6:14–16).
The Church is made from one material, the saints (I Pt. 2:5).

All the Types and Shadows of the Old Testament

4. The Ark had one sealing agent, it was covered with pitch within and without (Gen. 6:14).

The Church has one authorized sealing agent, the blood of Christ (II Tim. 2:19; Jno, 6:27).

5. The Ark had but one light source (Gen. 6:16).

The Church has one light source, Jesus Christ (Jno 1:1–4; Heb. 1:1–2).

6. The Ark had but one door (Gen. 6:16).

The Church has but one door, entrance into the church can only be gained through Jesus Christ (John 10:7, 9).

7. The Ark provided the passage to safety, Mount Ararat (Gen. 8:4).

The Church of Christ provides passage to eternal safety of heaven, Mount Zion (Heb. 12:22-23).

8. The door of the Ark was on the side (Gen. 6:16).

The door of the Church (Jesus) was opened on His side (John 19:34).

9. The Ark had many rooms (Gen. 6:14).

The Church has many local congregations and many mansions (Jno 14:2-3).

10. The Ark was populated by just one family (Gen. 7:1).

The Church is populated by one family, the household of God (Eph. 2:19; Gal. 3:28–29).

11. Only the saved were in the Ark (Gen. 7:1).

Only the saved are in the Church (Acts 2:47; Heb. 2:10; Eph. 5:23).

The Ark: A Type of the Church

12. The lost died in the flood, outside the Ark (Gen. 6:13).

The lost will perish outside of the Church in the flood of sin (John 15:4).

13. Righteousness was found inside the Ark (Gen. 7:1).

Righteousness is found in the Church (I Pet 3:12; I Jno 5:13).

14. The ark (and those in it) was saved through waters of judgment (Gen. 7:17-23).

The church (and those in it) are saved through the waters of baptism (I Pet. 3:21).

All the Types and Shadows of the Old Testament

Noah:
A Type of Christ

Only a few men in the recorded history of the Scripture serve as a type of Christ. Those who do were men of great faith and obedience to the Lord. In Noah we see his great faith coupled with his full obedience to God's commands.

1. Noah found favor with God (Gen. 6:8).
Christ found favor with God (Luke 2:52; Matt. 3:17; 17:5).

2. Noah was a man (Gen. 6:9).
Christ was a man (I Tim. 2:5).

3. Noah walked with God (Gen. 6:9).
Jesus walked with God (John 8:29).

4. Noah was a carpenter (Gen. 6:9, 14-16).
Jesus was a carpenter (Mark 6:3; I Pet. 2:5).

5. Noah was captain of the Ark (Gen. 7:1).
Jesus is the captain of salvation (Heb. 2:10).

6. Noah alone was authorized to build the ark (Gen. 6:14).
Christ alone was authorized to build the church (Matt. 16:18; Heb. 3:3-6).

All the Types and Shadows of the Old Testament

7. Noah had a covenant with God (Gen. 6:18; Gen. 9:9).
Jesus has a covenant with man (Heb. 8:6; II Cor. 3:6).

8. Noah did all God commanded (Gen. 6:22).
Jesus did all God commanded (John 4:34).

9. Noah completed his task (Gen. 6:22).
Jesus completed his task (John 17:4).

10. Noah was a righteous man (Gen. 7:1).
Jesus was righteous man (Luke 23:47).

11. Noah was head of his family (Gen. 7:1).
Jesus is head of the church (Eph. 1:22-23).

12. Noah was a preacher of righteousness, 2 Pet 2:5.
Jesus was a preacher of righteousness (Matt. 4:23).

13. Noah provided a place of safety for his family (Gen. 7:1).
Jesus provides a place of safety for His family (John 14:1–3).

14. Noah saved his family (Gen. 7:7).
Jesus saves His family (Heb. 7:25).

15. Noah and his family were sent from the ark to the earth (Gen. 8:16).
Jesus sends His family into all the world (Mark 16:15; Acts 1:8).

16. Noah offered a sacrifice to the Lord (Gen. 8:20, 22).
Jesus offered Himself as a sacrifice to the Lord (Heb. 7:27; 9:14).

Noah: A Type of Christ

17. God blessed Noah and his family (Gen. 9:1).
Jesus blesses His family (Eph. 1:3).

18. Noah was given a sign of a covenant (Gen. 9:12 - 17).
Jesus gave a better covenant (Heb. 8:6).

All the Types and Shadows of the Old Testament

The Flood:
A Type of Baptism

The universal flood of Noah's day paints a picture of baptism which hangs on the wall of time and needs observation. Regarding those who scoffed at the preaching of Noah and refused to obey the message of salvation, Peter wrote:

> *Which sometime were disobedient, when once the longsuffering of God waited in the days of Noah, while the ark was a preparing, wherein few, that is, eight souls were saved by water. The like figure whereunto even baptism doth also now save us (not the putting away of the filth of the flesh, but the answer of a good conscience toward God,) by the resurrection of Jesus Christ (I Pet. 3:20-21).*

While many comparisons have been observed with other things presented heretofore, the ark is one of a singular simplicity, yet one which forever settles the matter of the essentiality of baptism and salvation.

1. The flood of Noah's day was universally dispersed upon all men (Gen. 6:13).

The blood of Christ was universally dispersed for all men (Matt. 26:28; I John 2:2; John 1:29).

2. The flood of Noah's day saved those obedient to God. Gen. 6-9; Heb. 11:7.

Baptism saves those who obey the Lord (I Pet. 3:21; Acts 2:38).

All the Types and Shadows of the Old Testament

Job:
A Type of Christ

The number of skeptics who deny Job was a real man seems endless. Not a few insist the book of Job is simply parabolic and cannot be, therefore, considered or classified as factual.

A parable is a story of an account of something that could or did happen, which is meant to convey a deeper truth. There are four purposes of parables: *First,* a parable is to reveal truth. *Second,* a parable may conceal truth. *Third,* a parable embalms truth, that is, it preserves truth. *Fourth,* a parable is sometimes used to cause one to assent to truth without initially realizing the parable applies to him. Consider II Sam. 12:1–7.

There is positive proof Job was indeed an actual person. The prophet Ezekiel forever lays the matter to rest, saying: "*The word of the Lord came again to me, saying, Son of man, when the land sinneth against me by trespassing grievously, then will I stretch out mine hand upon it, and will break the staff of the bread thereof, and will send famine upon it, and will cut off man and beast from it: Though these three men, Noah, Daniel, and Job, were in it, they should deliver but their own souls by their righteousness, saith the Lord God*" (Eze. 14:12–14). Ezekiel's inspired words not only mentions Noah and Daniel as authentic, but Job as well.

One of the most astonishing remarks made by Job is recorded in Job 19:25–27, which reads: "*For I know that my redeemer liveth, and that he shall stand at the latter*

All the Types and Shadows of the Old Testament

day upon the earth: And though after my skin worms destroy this body, yet in my flesh shall I see God: Whom I shall see for myself, and mine eyes shall behold, and not another; though my reins be consumed within me." Job, by inspiration, knew there was a redeemer for men obedient to God's will; and even though that redeemer was yet to come, Job knew and believed in Him.

James, the Lord's brother, wrote of Job, saying: "*Behold, we count them happy which endure. Ye have heard of the patience of Job, and have seen the end of the Lord; that the Lord is very pitiful, and of tender mercy*" (Jas. 5:11). The word patience, as used by James, is defined as steadfastness, constancy, endurance or continuance. These four qualities are indeed observed in the characteristics of Job, and are worthy qualities for saints to emulate in their daily lives.

It is more than likely Abraham and Job were acquainted. Referring to the commentaries of Keil and Deiltzshch, Adam Clarke and Albert Barnes will assist the reader in this matter. The proofs these commentators supply are too voluminous to insert here, but it is hoped use of these works can and will be utilized.

Consider the number of ways the man Job serves as a ante-type of Christ.

1. Job's faith was tried and tested by his family (Job 2:9).
Christ was tested by his brethren (John 7:3-5).

2. Job was falsely accused of being a sinner by his friends (Job 4:4-9).
Christ was accused of being a sinner (Matt. 26:57–68).

Job: A Type of Christ

3. Job was a man of integrity (Job 27:5).
Christ was a man of integrity (Luke 2:40).

4. Job remained faithful to God (Job 27:5).
Christ remained faithful to God (Heb. 5:8-9; 4:15).

5. Job was tried by Satan (Job 1:6–2:10).
Christ was tried by Satan (Matt. 4:1–11; Luke 4:1–13.

6. Job lost all he had (Job. 1:13–22).
Christ gave up all He had in heaven (Phil. 2:5–11).

7. Job offered sacrifices on behalf of his family (Job 1:1–5).
Christ sacrificed Himself on behalf of mankind (Heb. 7:24–28).

8. Job was perfect (Job 1:1).
Christ was perfect (Heb. 4:15).

9. Job served as a mediator between God and men (Job 1:5).
Christ is the mediator between God and men (I Tim. 2:5).

10. Job suffered as a man of grief (Job 3).
Christ suffered as a man of grief (Isa. 53:10).

11. Job suffered physical affliction (Job 2:1–8).
Christ suffered physical affliction (Matt. 27:26–35).

12. Job prophesied of the resurrection (Job 19:25-26).
Christ prophesied of the resurrection (John 11:25).

All the Types and Shadows of the Old Testament

13. Job interceded for his friends (Job 42:7–10).

Jesus was raised up as our great Intercessor (Rom. 8:34; Heb. 7:25).

14. Job bore the marks of suffering on his body (Job. 2:7-8).

Christ bore the marks of suffering on His body (Luke 24:39).

Abraham:
A Type of Christ

In contrast to the few comparisons between the flood of Noah and baptism; in Abraham we have numerous comparative pictures on which to fasten our eyes. The artistic hand of God painted the following for consideration, which, when considered properly, aids one in better understanding the scenes of salvation set forth in the inspired record.

1. Abraham received God's promise (Gen. 12:1, 3).
Christ received God's promise (Acts 2:33; Psalm 110:4).

2. Abraham went into Egypt (Gen. 12:10).
Christ went into Egypt (Matt. 2:13, 15).

3. Abraham was very rich (Gen. 13:2).
Christ was very rich (Phil. 2:5, 11).

4. Abraham had a beautiful Bride (Gen. 12:11).
Christ has a beautiful Bride (Rev. 22:17; Eph. 5:25–27).

5. Abraham was given a new name Gen. 17:5.
Christ gives a new name (Acts 11:26; Isa. 62:2).

6. Abraham was given a sign of a covenant (Gen. 17:10-11).
Christ gives a seal of ownership (II Tim. 2:19).

All the Types and Shadows of the Old Testament

7. Abraham was visited by angels (Gen. 18:1, 21-22; 19:1).
Christ was visited by angels (Matt. 4:1, 11).

8. Abraham made intersession for his blood related family (Gen. 18:22-23).
Christ intercedes for His blood related family (I Tim. 2:5; Rom. 8:34).

9. Abraham's son was born by a miracle (Gen. 21:1-2).
Jesus, the Son of God, was born by miracle (Isa. 7:14; Matt. 1:18).

10. Abraham offered his son as sacrifice (Gen. 22:1-18).
Christ was a Son offered as a sacrifice (Isa. 53:1, 12; John 3:16).

11. Many blessed through Abraham (Gen. 12:1-3).
The Father blesses many through Christ (Eph. 1:3; Gal. 3:26, 29).

12. Abraham gave up the ghost (Gen. 25:8).
Christ gave up the ghost (Matt. 27:50; Mark 15:37; Luke 23:46).

13. Abraham saved his blood relatives (Gen. 14:14-16).
Christ saves His blood relatives (I Tim. 2:6; Rom. 6:11).

14. Abraham was blessed by kings (Gen. 14:18-19; Heb. 7:1).
Christ blesses kings (I Tim 2:2).

15. Abraham was given a great name (Gen. 12:1, 3).
Christ was given a great name (Phil. 2:9).

Abraham: A Type of Christ

16. Abraham was promised a seed child (Gen. 12:1, 3).
Christ is the promised seed child (Gal. 3:16).

17. Abraham's seed promised to be innumerable (Gen. 12:1, 3).
Christ's seed is innumerable (Rev. 7:9).

18. Abraham served the King of Most High (Gen. 14:22).
Christ is the King Most High (Zech. 6:12-13; Dan. 7:13-14; Acts 2:30, 35).

19. Abraham's belief was accounted as righteousness (Gen. 15:6).
Christ's obedient believers are righteous (Matt. 6:33; John 7:24; Rom. 4:5).

20. Abraham made a covenant with God (Gen. 17:9-14).
Christ made New Covenant with man (Jer. 31:31-34; Heb. 8:8-13).

21. Abraham was promised twelve princes to come from his seed (Gen. 17:20).
Christ made the apostles rulers put on twelve thrones (Matt. 19:28).

22. Abraham's children were obedient to him (Gen. 18:19).
Christ's children are obedient Him (Heb. 5:8-9).

23. Abraham had a blessed bride (Gen. 20:16; 21:1-2).
Christ's bride is blessed (Eph. 1:3).

All the Types and Shadows of the Old Testament

24. Abraham made purchase for bride's death (Gen. 23:1-2, 16-20).
Christ made purchase for bride's life (Acts 20:28).

25. Abraham sent his servant to find a bride (Gen. 24:1-4).
Christ came to buy a bride (John 3:16; Eph 5:22, 27).

26. Abraham gave all to his son (Gen. 25:5).
Christ was the Son to whom all is given (Matt. 28:18; I Cor. 15:24; Eph. 1:22).

27. Abraham came out of Egypt (Gen. 12:10-20; 13:1).
Christ came out of Egypt , Matt. 2:14-15.

28. Abraham had an only begotten son (Gen. 22:2; Heb. 11:17).
Christ is the only begotten son of God (John 3:16).

29. Abraham loved His only begotten son (Gen. 22:2).
Christ was the only begotten Son of God loved by the Father (Matt. 3:17; 17:5).

30. Abraham believed God could raise his son from the dead (Heb. 11:17-19).
Christ was raised from the dead by God (Rom. 1:4).

31. Abraham's wife was given a new name (Gen. 17:15).
Christ's wife is given a new name (Isa. 62:2; Acts 11:26).

32. Abraham looked for a city built by God (Heb. 11:10).
Christ is the builder of the city of God (John 14:2).

Abraham: A Type of Christ

33. Abraham receives the saved into his bosom in paradise (Luke 16:22).

Christ will receive the saved into His bosom in heaven (Matt. 25:31–34).

34. Abraham had his faith tried (Heb. 11:17).

Christ had His faith tried (Matt. 4:1–11).

35. Abraham left his home as commanded by God (Gen. 12:1).

Christ left his home as commanded by God (Gal. 4:4).

36. Abraham paid tithes to the king and priest of the Most High God (Gen. 14:18-20; Heb. 7:4–9).

Christ has contributions made to His church (I Cor. 16:1-2).

37. Abraham was called to leave his homeland and family (Gen. 12:1-3).

Jesus left heaven and His Father (Phil. 2:5-8).

All the Types and Shadows of the Old Testament

Melchizedek: A Type of Christ

Numerous passages mention Melchizedek who was both a King and priest of the Most High God in the city of Salem.

> And the king of Sodom went out to meet him after his return from the slaughter of Chedorlaomer, and of the kings that were with him, at the valley of Shaveh, which is the king's dale. And Melchizedek king of Salem brought forth bread and wine: and he was the priest of the most high God. And he blessed him, and said, Blessed be Abram of the most high God, possessor of heaven and earth: And blessed be the most high God, which hath delivered thine enemies into thy hand. And he gave him tithes of all (Gen. 14:17–20).

The following passages record several facts about Melchizedek, which clearly shows him to be a type of Christ:

> The Lord hath sworn, and will not repent, Thou art a priest for ever after the order of Melchizedek (Psa. 110:4).

> As he saith also in another place, Thou art a priest for ever after the order of Melchisedec. Who in the days of his flesh, when he had offered up prayers and supplications with strong crying and tears unto him that was able to save him from death, and was heard in that he feared; Though he were a Son, yet learned he obedience by the things which he suffered; And being made perfect, he became the author of eternal salvation unto all

All the Types and Shadows of the Old Testament

them that obey him; Called of God an high priest after the order of Melchisedec (Heb. 5:6–10).

For when God made promise to Abraham, because he could swear by no greater, he sware by himself, Saying, Surely blessing I will bless thee, and multiplying I will multiply thee. And so, after he had patiently endured, he obtained the promise. For men verily swear by the greater: and an oath for confirmation is to them an end of all strife. Wherein God, willing more abundantly to shew unto the heirs of promise the immutability of his counsel, confirmed it by an oath: That by two immutable things, in which it was impossible for God to lie, we might have a strong consolation, who have fled for refuge to lay hold upon the hope set before us: Which hope we have as an anchor of the soul, both sure and stedfast, and which entereth into that within the veil; Whither the forerunner is for us entered, even Jesus, made an high priest for ever after the order of Melchisedec (Heb. 6:13–20).

For this Melchisedec, king of Salem, priest of the most high God, who met Abraham returning from the slaughter of the kings, and blessed him; To whom also Abraham gave a tenth part of all; first being by interpretation King of righteousness, and after that also King of Salem, which is, King of peace; Without father, without mother, without descent, having neither beginning of days, nor end of life; but made like unto the Son of God; abideth a priest continually. Now consider how great this man was, unto whom even the patriarch Abraham gave the tenth of the spoils. And verily they that are of the sons of Levi, who receive the office of the priesthood, have a commandment to take tithes of the people according to the law, that is, of their brethren, though they come out of the

Melchizedek: A Type of Christ

loins of Abraham: But he whose descent is not counted from them received tithes of Abraham, and blessed him that had the promises. And without all contradiction the less is blessed of the better. And here men that die receive tithes; but there he receiveth them, of whom it is witnessed that he liveth. And as I may so say, Levi also, who receiveth tithes, payed tithes in Abraham. For he was yet in the loins of his father, when Melchisedec met him. If therefore perfection were by the Levitical priesthood (for under it the people received the law,) what further need was there that another priest should rise after the order of Melchisedec, and not be called after the order of Aaron? For the priesthood being changed, there is made of necessity a change also of the law. For he of whom these things are spoken pertaineth to another tribe, of which no man gave attendance at the altar. For it is evident that our Lord sprang out of Juda; of which tribe Moses spake nothing concerning priesthood. And it is yet far more evident: for that after the similitude of Melchisedec there ariseth another priest, Who is made, not after the law of a carnal commandment, but after the power of an endless life. For he testifieth, Thou art a priest for ever after the order of Melchisedec. For there is verily a disannulling of the commandment going before for the weakness and unprofitableness thereof. For the law made nothing perfect, but the bringing in of a better hope did; by the which we draw nigh unto God. And inasmuch as not without an oath he was made priest: (For those priests were made without an oath; but this with an oath by him that said unto him, The Lord sware and will not repent, Thou art a priest for ever after the order of Melchisedec). By so much was Jesus made a surety of a better testament. And they truly were many priests, because they

All the Types and Shadows of the Old Testament

were not suffered to continue by reason of death: But this man, because he continueth ever, hath an unchangeable priesthood. Wherefore he is able also to save them to the uttermost that come unto God by him, seeing he ever liveth to make intercession for them. For such an high priest became us, who is holy, harmless, undefiled, separate from sinners, and made higher than the heavens; Who needeth not daily, as those high priests, to offer up sacrifice, first for his own sins, and then for the people's: for this he did once, when he offered up himself. For the law maketh men high priests which have infirmity; but the word of the oath, which was since the law, maketh the Son, who is consecrated for evermore (Heb. 7:1–28).

1. Melchizedek was priest of the Most High God (Gen. 14:18).

Christ is our priest of the Most High God (Psa. 110:4; Heb. 5:5-10).

2. Melchizedek was the king of Salem (Jerusalem), Gen. 14:19.

Christ was anointed King over spiritual Jerusalem:

- Christ was anointed by both Deity and humanity, from head to foot.
- Anointed by Deity (Luke 4:18).
- Anointed by humanity on His head (Mark 14:3).
- Anointed by humanity on His feet (Luke 7:38).
- Anointed from heaven to show His authoritative power there (Matt. 28:18. I Cor. 15:24).
- Anointed on earth to show His authoritative power here (Matt. 28:18).

Melchizedek: A Type of Christ

3. Melchizedek blessed Abraham, who was in a right relationship with God (Gen. 14:18).

Christ blesses those who are in a right relationship with God (Eph. 1:3).

4. Melchizedek provided physical blessings to Abraham (Gen. 14:18).

Christ provides spiritual blessings to Abraham's seed (Eph. 1:3; Gal. 3:26, 29).

5. Melchizedek ruled in Salem (Jerusalem) (Heb. 7:1).

Christ rules from the heavenly Jerusalem (Heb. 12:2, 22-23).

6. Melchizedek was a king of peace (Heb. 7:2).

Christ is the king of peace (Isa. 9:6; Col. 1:20-21).

7. Melchizedek was a king of righteousness (Heb. 7:2).

Christ is a king of righteousness (I John 2:29).

8. Melchizedek was superior to Abraham (Heb. 7:4-7).

Christ is superior to Abraham (John 8:58; Rev. 1:8).

9. The is no record of Melchizedek's beginning (Heb. 7:3).

Christ has no Divine beginning (Eph. 3:9; Micah 5:2).

10. There is no record of Melchizedek's death, ending his priesthood (Heb. 7:3).

Christ forever lives and serves as our continual priest (Heb. 7:3).

All the Types and Shadows of the Old Testament

11. Melchizedek was a priest and king at the same time (Gen. 14:18–20).

Christ is both priest and king at the same time (Psa. 110:4; Zech. 6:12-13; Dan. 7:13-14).

12. Melchizedek was a priest and king of the Most High God before the Mosaic Law was given.

Christ was made priest and king after the Mosaic Law ended (Col. 2:14-15; Heb. 7:12).

13. Melchizedek had tithes given to him by Abraham (Gen. 14:20).

Christ has monetary contributions given to His church (I Cor. 16:1).

14. Melchizedek's priesthood did not change (Psa. 110:4).

Christ's priesthood shall not change (Psa. 110:4).

15. Melchizedek was an earthly king (Gen. 14:18; Heb. 7:1-2).

Christ is the heavenly king (Luke 23:2-3; John 18:36).

17. Melchizedek had God's approval, Psa110:4.

Christ has God's approval (Matt. 17:5; 12:18).

18. Melchizedek had supreme authority of his kingdom (Gen. 14:18).

Christ has the supreme authority in His kingdom and on the earth (Matt. 28:18).

Isaac:
A Type of Christ

As has been the case with the pervious men, women and events presented in distinctive fashion, Isaac now stands before the reader as another type of Christ. It is clear Isaac serves as a type of Christ in over a dozen patterns.

1. Isaac was the seed child of promise.

> And I will bless them that bless thee, and curse him that curseth thee: and in thee shall all families of the earth be blessed (Gen. 12:3)

> And in thy seed shall all the nations of the earth be blessed; because thou hast obeyed my voice (Gen. 22:18).

Christ was the seed child of promise. Observe the following passages.

> And I will put enmity between thee and the woman, and between thy seed and her seed; it shall bruise thy head, and thou shalt bruise his heel (Gen. 3:15).

> Therefore the Lord himself shall give you a sign; Behold, a virgin shall conceive, and bear a son, and shall call his name Immanuel (Isa. 7:14).

> Not according to the covenant that I made with their fathers in the day that I took them by the hand to bring them out of the land of Egypt; which my covenant they brake, although I was an husband unto them, saith the Lord (Jer. 31:32).

All the Types and Shadows of the Old Testament

> *And speak unto him, saying, Thus speaketh the Lord of hosts, saying, Behold the man whose name is The Branch; and he shall grow up out of his place, and he shall build the temple of the Lord: Even he shall build the temple of the Lord; and he shall bear the glory, and shall sit and rule upon his throne; and he shall be a priest upon his throne: and the counsel of peace shall be between them both (Zech. 6:12-13).*

> *Now to Abraham and his seed were the promises made. He saith not, And to seeds, as of many; but as of one, And to thy seed, which is Christ (Gal. 3:16).*

> *But when the fulness of the time was come, God sent forth his Son, made of a woman, made under the law, To redeem them that were under the law, that we might receive the adoption of sons (Gal. 4:4-5).*

2. Isaac's birth came by miracle (Gen. 11:30; 17:17; 21:1-2; Rom. 4:19-21; 9:9; Heb. 11:4–19).

- The Birth of Isaac was three-fold miracle.
- Sarah was barren.
- Sarah was past the age of child bearing.
- Abraham was also past age to procreate.

Christ's birth came by miracle (Isa. 7:14; Matt. 1:18–25).

- The birth of Christ was a three-fold miracle.
- Mary was a virgin.
- That which Mary conceived was of the Holy Ghost.
- She bore the Son Of God.

3. Isaac's name means laughter or joy (Gen. 21:1–7).

Christ brought about the joy of salvation (Luke 2:8–14; Phil. 4:4).

Isaac: A Type of Christ

4. Isaac was named before he was born (Gen. 17:19).
Christ was named before He was born (Matt. 1:21; Luke 1:31; 2:21).

5. Isaac was offered as a sacrifice (Gen. 22:1–12).
Jesus was offered as a sacrifice (John 3:16; Rom. 5:8; 8:32).

6. Abraham did not spare Isaac in order to obey God (Gen. 22:1–12).
Christ was not spared by God in order to save man (John 3:16; Rom. 5:8; 8:32).

7. Abraham's son willingly submitted to being sacrificed (Gen. 22: 9).
Christ willingly submitted to being sacrificed to save man (John 10:17-18; II Cor. 5:21; 8:9; Luke 22:42).

8. Isaac bore the wood for the sacrifice of himself (Gen. 22:6).
Christ bore the cross to sacrifice Himself (John 19:17).

9. Isaac had a ram offered in his place (Gen. 22:13).
Christ was offered in the place of sinners (John 1:29; I Pet. 1:18–22; Rev. 13:8).

10. Isaac was returned to his father (Gen. 22:12; Heb. 11:17–19).
Christ returned to His Father; Acts 1:9–11; Phil. 2:5–11; Dan. 7:12–14.

11. Isaac was obedient to his father (Gen. 22:9).
Christ was obedient to His Father (Luke 2:49; John 4:34; 9:4).

All the Types and Shadows of the Old Testament

12. Isaac was given a promise from God (Gen. 26:1-4).
Christ received a promise from God (Acts 2:33).

13. Isaac was offered as a sacrifice on Mount Moriah (Gen. 22:2).
Christ was offered as a sacrifice on Mount Moriah (Zion, in Jerusalem), the place of the skull (Matt. 27:33; Mark 15:22; II Chron. 3:1).

14. Isaac gave up the ghost at his death (Gen. 35:29).
Christ gave up the ghost at his death (Mark 15:37).

The Sons of Hagar and Sarah: Allegorical Types of the Old Law and the New Law

The allegory of Hagar and Sarah is inclusive of many matters as declared by Paul in Galatians 4:21–31. It is essential to recall many of the Jews insisted the Law of Moses was to be kept in conjunction with the new Law of Christ. In this allegory, Paul sets forth numerous allegorical observations in order to disprove the assertion made by the Jews (cf. Acts 15:1–21). Here we find it needful to quote the argument Paul presented in Galatians three.

> *Tell me, ye that desire to be under the law, do ye not hear the law? For it is written, that Abraham had two sons, the one by a bondmaid, the other by a freewoman. But he who was of the bondwoman was born after the flesh; but he of the freewoman was by promise. Which things are an allegory: for these are the two covenants; the one from the mount Sinai, which gendereth to bondage, which is Hagar. For this Hagar is mount Sinai in Arabia, and answereth to Jerusalem which now is, and is in bondage with her children. But Jerusalem which is above is free, which is the mother of us all. For it is written, Rejoice, thou barren that bearest not; break forth and cry, thou that travailest not: for the desolate hath many more children than she which hath an husband. Now we, brethren, as Isaac was, are the children of promise. But as then he that was born after the flesh persecuted him that was born after the Spirit, even so it*

All the Types and Shadows of the Old Testament

> *is now. Nevertheless what saith the scripture? Cast out the bondwoman and her son: for the son of the bondwoman shall not be heir with the son of the freewoman. So then, brethren, we are not children of the bondwoman, but of the free (Gal. 4:21–31).*

Some important points of observation are necessary to consider here. First, the two sons of Abraham were of two different social ranks. Ishmael was from the social rank of bondage. Isaac was of the social rank of freedom. The birth of Ishmael came about because of the spiritual weakness of both Abraham and Sarah—that is after the flesh. Isaac, however was born fulfilling the promise God made to Abraham as recorded in Genesis 17:15–19.

Paul sets forth the allegorical typology of Hagar, who represents the Old Covenant of Moses. Paul, then explains Sarah represents the New Covenant of Christ.

Ishmael typifies the Jews and Isaac typifies the Lord's church of the New Testament. Just as the descendants of Ishmael persecuted the descendants of Isaac so the Jews of the first century persecuted the Lord's church.

Ishmael and Isaac both received an inheritance from Abraham, though extremely different. Ishmael received the inheritance of a slave, or bondman, while Isaac received the inheritance of a freeman. Ishmael's inheritance was bread and water which was the portion given to a slave as is recorded in Genesis 21:14. Isaac, in contrast to Ishmael, received all from Abraham (Gen. 25:5).

1. Hagar was a handmaid of bondage (Gen. 16:5). Sarah was a woman of freedom (Gen. 21:2).

Sons of Hagar and Sarah: Types of Old & New Law

2. Ishmael was born through the flesh (Gal. 4:22).

Isaac was born by promise (Gal. 4:23; Gen. 18:10–14; 21:2).

3. Ishmael was a son born in domestic bondage (Gen. 16:5, 15).

Isaac was born in domestic freedom (Gen. 18:10–14; 21:2).

4. Ishmael was a persecutor (Gen. 16:12; 21:9; Gal. 4:29).

Isaac was the one persecuted by Ishmael (Gal. 4:29; Gen. 21:9).

5. Ishmael received the inheritance of a slave; Gen. 21:14.

Isaac Inherited all from his father (Gen. 21:10; 25:5).

6. Ishmael was born because of the weakness of faith in both Abraham and Sarah (Gen 16:1–4).

Isaac was born in the full assurance of faith (Gen. 21:1–7

7. Hagar received no inheritance from Abraham, Gen. 21:10–12; Gal. 4:30-31).

Sarah had access to all Abrahm's possessions while she lived.

8. Sarah and Isaac remained in favor with both God and Abraham (Gen. 18:10–14; 21:12).

9. Hagar and Ismael represent the Old Law to which God put an end (Col. 2:14; Eph. 2:14–16; Rom. 7:4; Gal. 4:23–25).

Sarah and Isaac represent the New Law of Christ which

All the Types and Shadows of the Old Testament

will forever remain.

10. Remaining under the Old Law was to be eternally lost (Rom. 3:9; Heb. 10:4).
Obedience to the New Law of Christ provides eternal life (Matt. 25:34).

11. Ishmael received the inheritance of bondage (Gen 21:14).
Saints in the Lord's church receive the inheritance of freedom (Matt. 25:34).

Joseph: A Type of Christ

The good eye of faith observes Christ in the life of Joseph, son of Jacob. His birth is recorded in Genesis 30:24 and he is last mentioned in Zechariah 10:6. Truly Joseph has been awarded much space in the Word of God, which should spark the interest of every Bible student. Joseph's life portrays Christ in numerous ways.

1. Joseph was favored, and well beloved by his father (Gen. 37:3).

Christ was favored, and well beloved by His Father (Matt. 3:17; 17:5; John 3:16).

2. The life of Joseph was preserved when he was but a youth (Gen. 37:2, 27-28).

Christ's life was preserved in His infancy (Matt. 2:13–15).

3. Joseph ruled over His brethren (Gen. 45:1–8).

Christ rules over all men (Matt. 28:18; I Tim. 6:15; Rev. 17:14; 19:16).

4. Joseph was sent on a mission of mercy by his father (Gen. 37:12–14).

Christ was sent on a mission by His Father to save man (John 1:29; 3:17; Luke 19:10; I John 4:14).

5. Joseph was hated by his brethren (Gen. 37:1–5).

Christ was hated by His brethren (John 1:11; 7:5).

All the Types and Shadows of the Old Testament

6. Joseph was exalted to an office of high authority (Gen. 41:39–43).

Christ was exalted to an office of supreme authority (Phil. 2:9–11; Acts 2:33).

7. Joseph's name was changed (Gen. 41:45).

Christ changes names (Isa. 62:2; Acts 11:26).

8. Joseph was stripped of his garment (coat of many colors) (Gen. 37:18–36).

Christ was stripped of his garments (Matt. 27:35; Mark 15:24; John 19:23-24).

9. Joseph was sold for the Old Testament price of a slave, twenty pieces of silver (Gen. 37:23–28).

Christ was sold for the New testament price of a slave, thirty pieces of silver (Matt. 26:15; 27:3–5).

10. Joseph's brethren believed they had gotten rid of him (Gen. 37:28).

The Jews believed they had gotten rid of Christ (Mark 15:13-14; 29–31; Isa. 53:10–12).

11. Joseph's brethren had to face him later (Gen. chapters 42–44).

All men will have to face Christ at judgment (Acts 17:30-31; Rom. 14:12; Ecc. 12:14; Matt. 25:41–46).

12. Joseph's brethren lied about what became of him (Gen. 37:31–34).

The Jews lied about what became of Christ (Matt. 28:11–15).

Joseph: A Type of Christ

13. Joseph was tempted, but remained spiritually pure (Gen. 39:7–12).

Christ was tempted and remained sinless (Matt. 4:1–11; Heb. 4:15; I Pet. 2:22).

14. Joseph was thirty years old when he began his public work that saved many from death (Gen. 41:46).

Jesus was thirty years old when He began His public ministry to save many from spiritual death (Luke 3:23).

15. Joseph invited his brethren to come to him for food (Gen. 45:9–11; 50:15–21).

Christ invites all men to come to Him for spiritual food (John 4:10–14; 6:48).

16. Joseph forgave his brethren when they obeyed him (Gen. 45:1–15; 50:15–21).

Christ forgives men when they obey Him (Luke 24:24; Heb. 5:8-9).

17. Joseph gave his brethren the best of the land of Egypt (Gen. 45:10).

Christ will give obedient men the best of heaven (John 14:1–3; Heb. 4:9).

18. What Joseph's brethren meant for evil against him, God used for good (Gen. 50:20).

What Jesus' brethren (the Israelites) meant for evil against Him, God used for good (Acts 2:23).

19. In his death Joseph was returned to his home (Gen. 50:22–26; Exo. 13:19).

After the death of Christ He returned to His home (Dan. 7:13-14; Acts 1:9–11; Heb. 9:24).

All the Types and Shadows of the Old Testament

20. Joseph was buried under the oversight of Joshua (Joshua 24:31-32).

Jesus (whose name is the same as *Joshua*) was buried under the oversight of a man named Joseph (John 19:38-42).

21. Joseph was buried with honor and dignity (Gen. 50:26; Josh. 24:32; Heb. 11:22).

Christ was buried with honor and dignity (Matt. 27:57–60; Mark 15:44–46; Luke 23:52-53; John 19:38-42).

The Burning Bush: A Type of the Church

Moses spent forty years in Egypt and was adopted by the daughter of Pharoah when he was three months old. Moses fled to Midian after having killed an Egyptian, where he remained forty years. There he married the daughter of Jethro, priest of Midian. "And Moses was content to dwell with the man: and he gave Moses Zipporah his daughter" (Exo. 2:21). After forty years in Midian the Lord called Moses to return to Egypt and lead the Israelites out of Egypt. The Lord spoke to Moses from the burning bush:

> And the Lord said, I have surely seen the affliction of my people which are in Egypt, and have heard their cry by reason of their taskmasters; for I know their sorrows; And I am come down to deliver them out of the hand of the Egyptians, and to bring them up out of that land unto a good land and a large, unto a land flowing with milk and honey; unto the place of the Canaanites, and the Hittites, and the Amorites, and the Perizzites, and the Hivites, and the Jebusites (Exo. 3:7-8).

This event of the burning bush paints a clear picture of the church of the New Testament.

1. The Lord proclaimed His instructions and message to Moses to deliver the Israelites from Egyptian bondage (Exodus 3–4).

Today, the church proclaims the Lord's message, which can deliver sinful men from sin-bondage when obeyed.

All the Types and Shadows of the Old Testament

2. The ground upon which Moses stood was holy (Exo. 3:5; Acts 7:33).

The church stands on holy ground (I Pet. 2:9; I Tim. 3:15; Eph. 3:10, 21; 5:27; Heb. 10:19–22; I Cor. 11:17–34).

3. A bush was considered without value.

The church is, however, of great value but considered worthless and unimportant by most (Acts 2:47; 8:34; 20:28; Eph. 3:21; 5:25).

4. The burning bush was in the desert (Exo. 3:1–3).

The church is in the desert of sin (I John 5:19; Eph. 2:2).

5. The burning bush was not consumed (Exo. 3:2).

The church cannot be consumed by fiery trials or persecutions (Matt. 16:18; Acts 8:4; 14:21-22; I Pet. 4:12-13).

6. The burning bush had the Lord in the midst of it (Exo. 3:4; Acts 7:31).

The church has the Lord in her midst (Eph. 2:20–22).

7. The burning bush was a great sight (Exo. 3:3; Acts 7:31).

The Lord's church is a beautiful sight (Eph. 5:27; Col. 1:22).

Moses:
A Type of Christ

Of all the characters of the inspired record none are like Christ in type as Moses. God used Moses as a type unlike any others in the Old Testament. He did this for the purpose of painting a clear picture of the Lord in the life of Moses, predominately for the benefit of the Jews in order to aid them in accepting Jesus as the Christ, the Messiah and prophet of whom Moses spoke as recorded in Deuteronomy;

> *The Lord thy God will raise up unto thee a Prophet from the midst of thee, of thy brethren, like unto me; unto him ye shall hearken; According to all that thou desiredst of the Lord thy God in Horeb in the day of the assembly, saying, Let me not hear again the voice of the Lord my God, neither let me see this great fire any more, that I die not. And the Lord said unto me, They have well spoken that which they have spoken. I will raise them up a Prophet from among their brethren, like unto thee, and will put my words in his mouth; and he shall speak unto them all that I shall command him. And it shall come to pass, that whosoever will not hearken unto my words which he shall speak in my name, I will require it of him (Deut. 18:15–19).*

That Christ was "like unto" Moses is clear and without contest among honest Bible students. In Moses we can observe several parallels with Christ which are plainly detailed by the hand of inspiration.

All the Types and Shadows of the Old Testament

1. Moses was preserved in his infancy (Exo. 2:2–10; Acts 7:20; Heb. 11:23).
Christ was preserved in His infancy (Matt. 2:13–15; Hos. 11:1).

2. Moses was a goodly child (Exo. 2:2; Acts 7:20; Heb. 11:23).
Christ was a goodly child (Luke 2:40, 52).

3. Moses contended with evil adversaries (Exo. 7:4; 11).
Christ contended with Satan (Matt. 4:1–11; Mark 1:12–15; Luke 4:1–13).

4. Moses fasted forty days (Exo. 34:28; Deut. 9:9).
Christ fasted forty days (Matt. 4:2; Luke 4:2).

5. Moses was made a god (Exo. 7:1).
Christ is God (Matt. 1:23; John 1:1; Acts 20:28; Tit. 2:13; II Pet. 1:1; I John 5:20).

6. Moses controlled the Red Sea (Exo. 14:16, 21).
Christ controlled the Sea of Galilee (Mark 4:39).

7. Moses fed multitudes (Exo. 16:11–16).
Christ fed multitudes (Matt. 14:21; 15:38).

8. Moses' face became radiant (Exo. 34:29–35).
Jesus' face became radiant (Matt. 17:2).

9. Moses endured harsh murmurings (Exo. 14:11; 16:2, 8–9; 17:3–4; Num. 11:1–6; 14:1–4).
Christ endured harsh murmurings (Luke 5:30; 15:2; John 6:41, 61; 7:12, 32).

Moses: A Type of Christ

10. Moses was discredited by his family members; Num. 12:1.

Christ was discredited by his family members (John 7:5; Mark 3:21; 6:4).

11. Moses made intercessory prayers for the Jews (Exo. 32:32; 34:9; Num. 14:19).

Christ made intercessory prayers for the apostles and the world (John 17:20–22).

12. Moses spoke the oracles of the Father (Exo. 24:2-3; Deut. 5:5, 27; 18:18-19).

Christ spoke the oracles of the Father (John 6:68; 12:49-50).

13. Moses was aided by seventy helpers (Exo. 24:1–9; Num. 11:16-17).

Christ was aided by seventy helpers (Luke 10:1).

14. Moses instituted the memorial of the Passover (Exo. 12:14).

Christ instituted the memorial of His death (Matt. 26:26–28; Mark 14:22–25; Luke 22:14–23).

15. Moses appeared after his death (Matt. 17:3).

Christ appeared after His death (Matt. 28:1–6; Luke 24:6–8; Acts 1:3).

- There are no less the twelve post-resurrection appearances of Christ, including His appearance to Saul on the road to Damascus.

16. Moses used a rod in his service to God (Exo. 4:2, 17; 17:9; Num. 20:8-9).

Christ rules with a rod of iron (Rev. 2:27; 19:15).

All the Types and Shadows of the Old Testament

17. Moses delivered the people of God (Exo. 14:13, 30). Christ delivers His people (Matt. 25:34; Gal. 5:1; Col. 1:18).

18. Moses gave God's law to His people (Deut. 2:1). Christ His law to the whole world (Gal. 5:1; 6:2; I Cor. 9:21).

19. Moses ruled over twelve tribes (Exo. 24:1–4; 28:21). Christ rules over twelve tribes (Matt. 19:28; Jas. 1:1).

20. Moses did many miracles (Exo. 4:17). Christ did many miracles (John 21:25).

The Tabernacle: A Type of the New Testament Church

The last forty years of Moses' life were spent in the wilderness. Two of the forty years were spent at the base of Mount Sinai, from the top of which Moses received the Law. From the time Moses received the Law until the Jews departed from thence was two years. Before leaving Mount Sinai Moses was directed by the Lord to construct the tabernacle according to the pattern show to him in the mount as recorded in Exodus 40 and Hebrews 8:5.

The Lord appeared to Moses in the wilderness of Mount Horeb. It is vital to understand the Lord who appeared to Moses in a flame of fire which came out of the midst of a bush was Christ (Exo. 3:2). *In the third month, when the children of Israel were gone forth out of the land of Egypt, the same day came they into the wilderness of Sinai* (Exo. 19:1).

According to Deuteronomy 2:14 the Israelites wandered in the wilderness for a total of thirty-eight years. The total number of years in the wilderness was indeed forty, but two were spent at the base of Mount Sinai.

We learn from Exodus 35 that God inspired select men to make the tabernacle and all the furnishings thereof as well as all the items of fabric and animal skins.

> *And Moses said unto the children of Israel, See, the Lord hath called by name Bezaleel the son of*

All the Types and Shadows of the Old Testament

> *Uri, the son of Hur, of the tribe of Judah; And he hath filled him with the spirit of God, in wisdom, in understanding, and in knowledge, and in all manner of workmanship; And to devise curious works, to work in gold, and in silver, and in brass, And in the cutting of stones, to set them, and in carving of wood, to make any manner of cunning work. And he hath put in his heart that he may teach, both he, and Aholiab, the son of Ahisamach, of the tribe of Dan. Them hath he filled with wisdom of heart, to work all manner of work, of the engraver, and of the cunning workman, and of the embroiderer, in blue, and in purple, in scarlet, and in fine linen, and of the weaver, even of them that do any work, and of those that devise cunning work (Exo. 30:30–35).*

The required to time to complete their work was two years, after which Moses reared up the tabernacle: *And the Lord spake unto Moses, saying, On the first day of the first month shalt thou set up the tabernacle of the tent of the congregation* (Exo. 40:1-2). Some may have objection to Moses setting up the Tabernacle alone. However, just as the Lord endowed certain men to fabricate the Tabernacle and the furnishings thereof He endowed Moses with the fortitude to assemble the Tabernacle by himself.

Just as Moses typified Christ in numerous ways, the Tabernacle and the furnishings thereof typify the New Testament church in numerous ways. It is a difficult thing to close the eye of ignorance and skepticism regarding the clarity God painted for us of the many things which furnished the Tabernacle.

Moses was given detailed instructions for the construction of the Tabernacle during his forty days and nights atop Mount Sinai, in addition to the Law of God for the

The Tabernacle: A Type of the Church

Jews as recorded in Exo. 25:40. The Lord provided a clear vision to Moses of how the Tabernacle was to be constructed, as Stephen said: *Our fathers had the tabernacle of witness in the wilderness, as he had appointed, speaking unto Moses, that he should make it according to the fashion that he had seen* (Acts 7:44). Further, the Hebrew author tells us: *Moses was admonished of God when he was about to make the tabernacle: for, See, saith he, that thou make all things according to the pattern shewed to thee in the mount* (Heb. 8:5).

The figure below shows the locations of all the Tabernacle furnishings. This is presented for astute consideration. Each of the Tabernacle furnishings serve as types of what is found in the Lord's New Testament church.

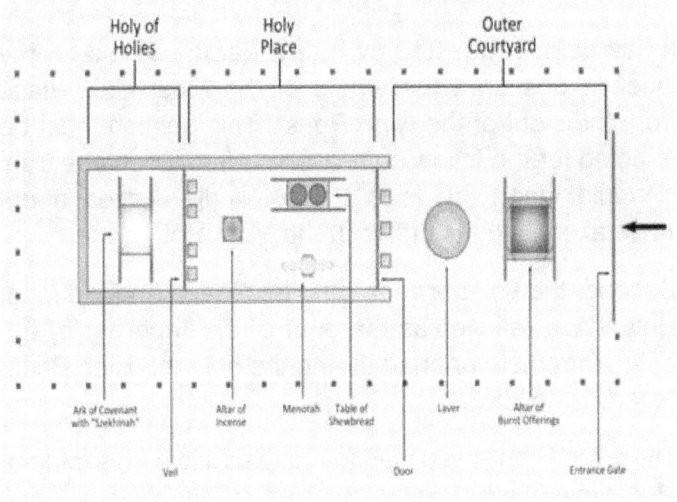

We are compelled to address the difficulty which arises regarding the text of Hebrews 9, which reads: *And after*

All the Types and Shadows of the Old Testament

the second veil, the tabernacle which is called the Holiest of all; Which had the golden censer, and the ark of the covenant overlaid round about with gold, wherein was the golden pot that had manna, and Aaron's rod that budded, and the tables of the covenant (Heb. 9:3-4).

Some contend the censer mentioned here was a part of the furnishings of the Most Holy Place and remained there. Others insist the censer was taken into the Most Holy Place and then removed by the High Priest once his required duties were completed in the Most Holy Place. Regardless, it was used to contain some of the incense taken from the altar of incense which was just before the veil of the Most Holy Place. Regarding matters of opinion we must not be contentious, but rather tolerant, so long as any given opinion does not blithe the Word of the Lord.

It has been suggested by many that the smoke of the incense obscured the whole of the Most Holy Place from the sight of the High Priest. This opinion must be rejected for the following reasons: First, if such be true, it would mean the High Priest blindly walked about while executing his duties in the Most Holy place.

Second, the veil between the Holy Place and the Most Holy Place (as well as the door of the Tabernacle) appears to remain opened during the time the High Priest entered into it.

Third, the High Priest was to make multiple trips into the Most Holy Place. The first, was to "*put the incense upon the fire before the Lord, that the cloud of the incense may cover the mercy seat.*" Another entrance into the Most Holy Place was with the blood of a bullock. Another was with the blood of a goat. The High Priest was

The Tabernacle: A Type of the Church

to "*put the incense upon the fire before the Lord, that the cloud of the incense may cover the mercy seat that is upon the testimony, that he die not: And he shall take of the blood of the bullock, and sprinkle it with his finger upon the mercy seat eastward; and before the mercy seat shall he sprinkle of the blood with his finger seven times. then shall he kill the goat of the sin offering, that is for the people, and bring his blood within the vail, and do with that blood as he did with the blood of the bullock, and sprinkle it upon the mercy seat, and before the mercy seat*" (Lev. 16:13–15).

It is clear at least three trips were made into the Most Holy Place by the High Priest. We must deduce the High Priest made another trip into the Most Holy Place to retrieve the censer of ashes once the incense was consumed. In his commentary on Hebrews chapter nine, verses six through ten, Robert Milligan wrote, concerning the High Priest that he went into the Most Holy Place:

> ... once a year, on the tenth day of the seventh month. But on that day he entered the Most Holy Place at least three times, perhaps four. This will be best explained by indicating briefly the varied services of that most solemn of all the days of the year, as given in the sixteenth chapter of Leviticus. After the usual morning services and the offering of the sacrifices prescribed in Num. xxix. 7–11, the High Priest was required (1) to kill the bullock which he had provided for a sin-offering for himself and for his house (Lev. xvi. 11); (2) to carry a pan of coals from the Brazen Altar and also a portion of sweet incense into the Most Holy Place, and there to burn the incense before the Lord (vv. 12-13); (3) to enter the second time with the blood of the bullock, and to sprinkle it

All the Types and Shadows of the Old Testament

seven times on and before the Mercy Seat (v. 14); (4) to slay the goat of the sin-offering for the people (v. 15); (5) to go the third time within the Vail, with the blood of this goat, and to do with it as he had done with the blood of the bullock.

We feel obligated to address the notion made by many, that the High Priest was to have a rope tied to his ankle in the event the High Priest were to be smitten by the Lord and die while in the Most Holy Place. We insist the suggestion is not at all true. Moses wrote: "*And there shall be no man in the tabernacle of the congregation when he goeth in to make an atonement in the holy place, until he come out, and have made an atonement for himself, and for his household, and for all the congregation of Israel*" (Lev. 16:17).

Further, if it were the case the High Priests were required to have such a tethering, should we not deduce such a tether would have been identified and revealed to Moses during his time on the mount when he received the Lord's instructive pattern for all things pertaining to the Tabernacle? We read of no such tethering device anywhere in the Scripture.

It has further argued the bells round about the hem of the garment of the High Priest (Exo. 28:33; 39:25) were for the purpose of allowing those outside the Tabernacle to hear the activity of the High Priest. This too, must be rejected on the basis there is not so much as one syllable in any inspired text to support the opinion. If so, where is the passage found? Indeed numerous opinions have become standards which govern many. The number of types found in the Tabernacle of Moses is many and warrants a studious eye.

The Tabernacle: A Type of the Church

1. When considering the Tabernacle of Moses it is clear there was but one (Exo. 40:2).

There is but one New Testament church (Matt. 16:18; Eph. 1:22-23; Col. 1:18).

2. There was only one builder of the Tabernacle, Moses (Exo. 40:1-2, 33).

There was but one builder of the Lord's church, that is Christ (Zech. 6:12; 13: Matt. 16:18; Heb. 3:3-6).

3. There was one Divinely given set of rules by which the Tabernacle was made (Exo. 25:9, 40; Heb. 8:5).

There is but one Divinely authorized pattern for the New Testament church (Acts 2:42).

- Christ as the head of the church (Eph. 1:22).
- Elders (I Tim. 3:1–7).
- Deacons (I Tim. 3:8–13).
- Preachers (Eph. 4:11).
- Members (Acts 2:41, 47; Rom. 12:4-5).

4. There was but one door of the Tabernacle of Moses (See figure, p. 65).

There is but one door by which one can access the Lord's church (John 10:7–9).

5. The Tabernacle was governed by one set of rules (Num. 15:16, 23).

The Lord's church is governed by one set of rules (Acts 2:42; Phil. 2:2; 3:16).

6. Once completed the glory of the Lord appeared in the Tabernacle (Exo. 40:34–38).

The glory of the Lord is found only in the church (Eph. 1:17–23; I Cor. 2:8; Rev. 7:12).

All the Types and Shadows of the Old Testament

7. Only the Levites were granted access into the Holy Place (Num. 1:53; 3:6–9; 18:1–6).

Only obedient baptized believers of the gospel are granted access into the Lord's church (Acts 2:47; I Cor. 1:2; 12:13; Col. 3:15).

8. There was only one light source in the Holy Place, the golden candlestick, which represents the Word of God (Exo. 25:37; Num. 8:2).

- Oil for the candlestick was of a specific order. Beaten out and not extracted by heat, when the oil flowed out by itself was of the finest quality and color (Exo. 27:20).

There is but one light in the Lord's church (John 1:4; 8:12; Acts 13:47; 26:23).

- Christians are to walk in the light (I John 1:5–7; Eph. 5:8).

9. There was but one anointing oil for the Tabernacle and all the furnishings thereof; Exo. 30:31–38; Lev. 8:10).

The church has but one anointing blood, that of Christ (Eph. 2:13; Heb. 9:14; I Pet. 1:19).

10. Moses' radiant face represents Christ (Exo. 34:29–35).

Christ's face became radiant; Matt. 17:1-2; Acts 26:13–15.

11. There was but one altar of sacrifice for the Tabernacle, which represents the cross of Christ (Exo. 27:1–8).

There is but one cross upon which the Lord was sacrificed (Matt. 27:32–44).

The Tabernacle: A Type of the Church

- There were three crosses on Golgotha:
- One cross represents one who died in sin.
- One cross represents one who died to sin.
- One cross represents the one who died for sin.

12. The altar was outside of the Holy Place for all to see and to which all were to come (Exo. 40:6).

The cross of Christ was outside the city for all to see and to which all must come (Heb. 13:12; Isa. 53:8; John 19:17-18).

13. There was but one type of authorized sacrificial animal to sacrifice on the altar, one which was without blemish, which represents Christ (Lev. 1:3, 10; 3:1).

Christ was the only sacrifice authorized by the Father (Rom. 5:8–11; I Pet. 1:19).

14. The sacrifice had to be voluntary offered (Lev. 1:3; 7:16).

Christ sacrificed Himself voluntarily and willingly (John 10:15; 10:17; 10:18).

15. The laver in which the priests were to wash before entering the Holy Place was outside the door (see figure, p. 65), Exo. 30:18; 40:30.

Baptism is a washing which must be performed before one is granted entrance to the Lord's church (Mark 16:15-16; Acts 2:41; I Pet. 3:21; Gal. 3:26-27).

- In every passage of the New Testament in which baptism is recorded, God's blessings of cleansing, rejoicing and forgiveness always comes *after* baptism.
- Baptism has always stood between salvation and damnation, and between blessings and consequences.

All the Types and Shadows of the Old Testament

- The word *baptism* is found in twenty-two passages of the New Testament, *baptized* is found in fifty-one verses, and *baptizing* is recorded in four passages.

16. The Holy Place was entered only by the Priests (Exo. 27:21; 29:44).

Only Christians (New Testament priests, I Pet. 2:5, 9), are in the Holy Place of the church (Acts 2:47).

17 The golden candlestick was in the Holy Place to provide light (Exo. 40:4; 24-25; 25:6, 37; 26:35).
- The candlestick was a type of the Word of God (Psa. 119:105).
- The candlestick had a specific recipe for the oil used (Exo. 27:20).

Only in the Lord's church is found light to the world (Phi. 2:15-16; I Pet. 2:9).

18. The table of shewbread upon which was placed twelve loaves of unleavened was reserved for the Levites who served in the Holy Place (Lev. 24:5–9).

The twelve loaves represents the Lord's Supper in type.

- Lord's church (Matt. 26:26–29; I Cor. 11:23–25).
- The showbread was unleavened (Lev. 2:4).
- The bread used for the Lord's Supper is unleavened, it was used when the Lord instituted His memorial (Luke 22:1–7; Mark14:1–11).

19. The altar of incense was found only in the Holy Place (Exo. 40:4, 17, 26).
- The incense was carried by the High Priest into the Most Holy Place where the Mercy Seat of God was located (Lev. 16:12-13).
- The incense was made of a restricted recipe

The Tabernacle: A Type of the Church

(Exo. 30:34–38).

The prayers of the saints, found only in the in the Lord's church, are a sweet incense of the Lord, and clearly connected to the altar of incense in Rev. 8:3-4.

- Christ, our High Priest takes the prayers of the saints before the Father (I Tim. 2:5; Rev. 8:3-4).
- These prayers are only those of the children of God (John 9:31).

20. The veil between the Holy and Most Holy Place represents both death and Christ.

- Represents Christ in that all must go through Christ to obtain heaven; John 14:6; Acts 4:12; I Cor. 15:50–54.
- Represents death in that all must die before entering heaven, except for those who alive and remain at the second coming of Christ; (I Thes. 4:13–18); Heb. 9:27.

21. The sealed Ark of the Covenant in the Most Holy Place represents God forever sealing His word (Exo. 32:18; Psa. 119:89; Matt. 24:34-35).

22. The Mercy Seat represents the throne of God (Exo. 25:21-22).

23. The Levites represents the Christian (Exo. 19:5-6; I Pet. 2:5, 9).

24. The High Priest represents Christ, our High Priest (Heb. 3:1; 4:15; 5:5-6; 7:11–26; Heb. 8:1; 9:11).

25. Only the High Priest was to enter the Most Holy Place (Heb. 4:14).

Only Christ has entered the Most Holy Place of heaven

All the Types and Shadows of the Old Testament

(Heb. 8:1-2).

26. The laver of Moses Tabernacle represents baptism.
- Placed between the door of the Tabernacle and the outer court (see figure, p. 65).
- Baptism stands between alien sinners and the church (Acts 2:28,; Eph. 5:26-27; I Pet. 3:21).
- Baptism puts on into the church. Rom. 6:3, 6; Gal. 3:26-27.

27. The Most Holy Place, which was a type of Heaven where God resides, was veiled in darkness (Exo. 33:20; Lev. 16:17).
- When the High Priest entered the Most Holy Place the veil between the Holy and Most Holy places likely remained open in order to provide enough light for the High Priest to conduct his duties.

Heaven is obscure and hidden from our view (John 1:18; 6:46; Col. 3:4; I John 3:2).

28. The ark of the covenant contained the two tables of stone which represented the sealing of God's word in heaven (Psa. 89:34; 119:89).

The New Testament was sealed by the blood of Christ and cannot be altered (Matt. 26:28. I Cor. 11:25; Heb. 13:20).

29. A golden pot of manna was inside the ark of the covenant as a reminder God provided earthly food for His people (Exo. 16:33; Heb. 9:4).

Christ is the spiritual food God provided for men (John 6:33–35; 41; 48).

The Tabernacle: A Type of the Church

30. Aaron's budding rod was placed in the ark of the covenant and represented Christ's scepter and rod (Num. 17:10).

The rod of Christ is the scepter He holds in heaven to govern the church (Rev. 12:5; 19:15).

31. The outer court represents the world.
- David introduced instrumental music into worship, but the use of said instruments was never used inside the temple itself (the Holy Place or Most Holy Place), but was limited to outside the actual temple (II Chro. 29:20-26).
- The outer court represents the world, which was the only place they could be used.
- The use of mechanical instruments is not authorized in the Lord's church, but they are used in worldly worship by those outside the church.
- The Lord tolerated the use of mechanical instrument for time, but demanded it to cease during the time of the prophet Amos (Amos 6:1–5).

All the Types and Shadows of the Old Testament

Egypt: A Type of Bondage in Sin and Spiritual Death

While the children of Israel were under the bondage of the Egyptians they were made to work *with rigor* as recorded in Exo. 1:13. *Rigor* means severity and cruel hardness. No little hardness and meanness was shown to the children of Israel under the decree of Pharaoh.

> *Therefore they did set over them taskmasters to afflict them with their burdens. And they built for Pharaoh treasure cities, Pithom and Ramses. But the more they afflicted them, the more they multiplied and grew. And they were grieved because of the children of Israel. And the Egyptians made the children of Israel to serve with rigor: And they made their lives bitter with hard bondage, in mortar, and in brick, and in all manner of service in the field: all their service, wherein they made them serve, was with rigor (Exo. 1:11–14).*

The degree and severity of the rigor with which the Israelites were made to serve not only inflicted physical abuses upon them, but also deep emotional strain.

Satan is well aware when children of God are endowed with strength and steadfastness, and he makes enormous efforts to inflict them with crafty wiles of every variety. Strong saints are most assaulted by the wicked one, those weak in the faith are less assaulted, but are assaulted nonetheless. However, Satan makes every effort to weaken the strongholds of the righteous. Pharaoh, like Satan, knew the "children of Israel are more and mightier" than the Egyptians and therefore "...said

All the Types and Shadows of the Old Testament

unto his people, Behold, the people of the children of Israel are more and mightier than we" (Exo. 1:9) and made the lives of the children of Israel "bitter with hard bondage" (Exo. 1:13).

1. The children of Israel were in bondage to Egypt.
Humans are in bondage to sin.

2. If the Israelites remained in bondage in Egypt, they would have been subject to physical death there.
Sinners who remain in the bondage of sin are subject to spiritual death (Rev. 2:10).

- So long as Satan is able to keep men in the bondage of sin he wins his war against the soul.

3. Israel was subject to Pharoah (Exo. 1).
Sinners are subject to Satan (I Cor. 6:9-11; Tit. 3:3; I Pet. 4:2; Eph 2:2).

4. The Taskmasters of the Israelites were cruel and harsh (Exo. 1:11–22).
Satan as taskmaster over sinners makes their life hard (Psa. 9:17; Pro. 13:15; II Tim. 2:26).

5. Moses was sent by God to save Israel (Exo. 3:1–10).
Christ was sent by God to save sinners (John 3:16-17; Rom. 5:8-9; I John 4:14).

6. Israel was required to believe and obey Moses (Exo. 4:1, 31).
Sinners must believe and obey Christ (John 3:16, 36; John 8:21, 24,

Egypt: A Type of Bondage in Sin

7. Israel was required to cease obeying Pharoah and obey Moses, Exo. 4:29–31).

Sinners must stop obeying their father the Devil and obey Christ (John 8:44; Matt. 6:24; Luke 13:3, 5; Acts 3:19; 17:30).

8. Israel was baptized unto Moses in the Red Sea (Exo. 14:30; I Cor. 10:1-2; Heb. 11:29).

Sinners must be baptized into Christ (Rom. 6:3-4; Gal. 3:26–29).

9. Israel was delivered from Pharoah when they were baptized in the Red Sea (Exo. 14:21–31; I Cor. 10:1-2).

Sinners are delivered from Satan when they are baptized (Acts 2:38; Mark 16:15-16; I Pet. 3:21).

10. Israel rejoiced and sang songs of praise when they were baptized (Exo. 15).

Saints rejoice when they obtain salvation (Acts 8:38-39; 16:30–34).

11. The Law of Moses was given from a mountain (Mt. Sinai), Exo. 20; Deut. 5; Acts 7:38.

The Law of Christ was given from a mountain (Mt. Zion), Isa. 2:2, 4; Mic. 4:1–3; Luke 24:46–48.

12. Israel was given physical food, Manna, to sustain them (Exo. 16:4).

Christians are given the spiritual food of Christ to sustain them (John 6:48).

13. Israel was provided physical water (Exo. 17:6).

Christians are provided the spiritual water of Christ (John 4:1–14).

All the Types and Shadows of the Old Testament

14. Many Israelites died in the wilderness (Num. 16:49; 25:9; I Cor. 10:5–10).

Many Christians apostatize and die in sin (Heb. 3:12; 6:4–6; I Cor. 10:4–13).

15. Canaan was the promised land for Israel (Gen. 13:15–17; 15:1–7; Psa. 105:11).

Christians have heaven as their promised land (John 14:1–3; Matt. 25:34; Heb. 11:10, 16).

Israelite Homes During the Death of the Firstborn: A Type of the Church

There are several matters to consider regarding the homes of the Israelites during the final plague—death of the firstborn. First, it is well to observe the mandates given by the Lord to Moses as recorded in Exodus 12:1–20.

Secondly, Moses repeats the Lord's instructions to the Israelites regarding the Passover Lamb, its blood, the side posts of the homes of the Israelites, and the mandate to remain in their houses during the time the destroyer passed through the land of Egypt.

> Then Moses called for all the elders of Israel, and said unto them, Draw out and take you a lamb according to your families, and kill the passover. And ye shall take a bunch of hyssop, and dip it in the blood that is in the bason, and strike the lintel and the two side posts with the blood that is in the bason; and none of you shall go out at the door of his house until the morning (Exo. 12:21-22).

Keil and Delitzsch provided the following comment:

> The reason for the command not to go out of the door of the house was, that in this night of judgment there would be no safety anywhere except behind the blood-stained door.[1]

---

[1] Keil and Delitzsch.

All the Types and Shadows of the Old Testament

And the Lord said unto Moses, Yet will I bring one plague more upon Pharaoh, and upon Egypt; afterwards he will let you go hence: when he shall let you go, he shall surely thrust you out hence altogether. Speak now in the ears of the people, and let every man borrow of his neighbour, and every woman of her neighbour, jewels of silver, and jewels of gold. And the Lord gave the people favor in the sight of the Egyptians. Moreover the man Moses was very great in the land of Egypt, in the sight of Pharaoh's servants, and in the sight of the people.

And Moses said, Thus saith the Lord, About midnight will I go out into the midst of Egypt: And all the firstborn in the land of Egypt shall die, from the firstborn of Pharaoh that sitteth upon his throne, even unto the firstborn of the maidservant that is behind the mill; and all the firstborn of beasts. And there shall be a great cry throughout all the land of Egypt, such as there was none like it, nor shall be like it any more. But against any of the children of Israel shall not a dog move his tongue, against man or beast: that ye may know how that the Lord doth put a difference between the Egyptians and Israel. And all these thy servants shall come down unto me, and bow down themselves unto me, saying, Get thee out, and all the people that follow thee: and after that I will go out. And he went out from Pharaoh in a great anger.

And the Lord said unto Moses, Pharaoh shall not hearken unto you; that my wonders may be multiplied in the land of Egypt. And Moses and Aaron did all these wonders before Pharaoh: and the Lord hardened Pharaoh's heart, so that he would not let the children of Israel go out of his land.

And the Lord spake unto Moses and Aaron in

Israelite Homes During the Death of the Firstborn

the land of Egypt, saying, This month shall be unto you the beginning of months: it shall be the first month of the year to you. Speak ye unto all the congregation of Israel, saying, In the tenth day of this month they shall take to them every man a lamb, according to the house of their fathers, a lamb for an house: And if the household be too little for the lamb, let him and his neighbour next unto his house take it according to the number of the souls; every man according to his eating shall make your count for the lamb. Your lamb shall be without blemish, a male of the first year: ye shall take it out from the sheep, or from the goats: And ye shall keep it up until the fourteenth day of the same month: and the whole assembly of the congregation of Israel shall kill it in the evening. And they shall take of the blood, and strike it on the two side posts and on the upper door post of the houses, wherein they shall eat it. And they shall eat the flesh in that night, roast with fire, and unleavened bread; and with bitter herbs they shall eat it. Eat not of it raw, nor sodden at all with water, but roast with fire; his head with his legs, and with the purtenance thereof. And ye shall let nothing of it remain until the morning; and that which remaineth of it until the morning ye shall burn with fire. And thus shall ye eat it; with your loins girded, your shoes on your feet, and your staff in your hand; and ye shall eat it in haste: it is the Lord's Passover. For I will pass through the land of Egypt this night, and will smite all the firstborn in the land of Egypt, both man and beast; and against all the gods of Egypt I will execute judgment: I am the Lord. And the blood shall be to you for a token upon the houses where ye are: and when I see the blood, I will pass over you, and the plague shall not be upon you to destroy you, when I smite the land of Egypt. And this day shall be unto you

All the Types and Shadows of the Old Testament

for a memorial; and ye shall keep it a feast to the Lord throughout your generations; ye shall keep it a feast by an ordinance for ever. Seven days shall ye eat unleavened bread; even the first day ye shall put away leaven out of your houses: for whosoever eateth leavened bread from the first day until the seventh day, that soul shall be cut off from Israel. And in the first day there shall be an holy convocation, and in the seventh day there shall be an holy convocation to you; no manner of work shall be done in them, save that which every man must eat, that only may be done of you And ye shall observe the feast of unleavened bread; for in this selfsame day have I brought your armies out of the land of Egypt: therefore shall ye observe this day in your generations by an ordinance for ever. In the first month, on the fourteenth day of the month at even, ye shall eat unleavened bread, until the one and twentieth day of the month at even. Seven days shall there be no leaven found in your houses: for whosoever eateth that which is leavened, even that soul shall be cut off from the congregation of Israel, whether he be a stranger, or born in the land. Ye shall eat nothing leavened; in all your habitations shall ye eat unleavened bread.

Then Moses called for all the elders of Israel, and said unto them, Draw out and take you a lamb according to your families, and kill the Passover. And ye shall take a bunch of hyssop, and dip it in the blood that is in the bason, and strike the lintel and the two side posts with the blood that is in the bason; and none of you shall go out at the door of his house until the morning. For the Lord will pass through to smite the Egyptians; and when he seeth the blood upon the lintel, and on the two side posts, the Lord will pass over the door, and will not suffer the destroyer to come in unto your

Israelite Homes During the Death of the Firstborn

> houses to smite you. And ye shall observe this thing for an ordinance to thee and to thy sons for ever. And it shall come to pass, when ye be come to the land which the Lord will give you, according as he hath promised, that ye shall keep this service. And it shall come to pass, when your children shall say unto you, What mean ye by this service? That ye shall say, It is the sacrifice of the Lord's Passover, who passed over the houses of the children of Israel in Egypt, when he smote the Egyptians, and delivered our houses.
>
> And the people bowed the head and worshiped And the children of Israel went away, and did as the Lord had commanded Moses and Aaron, so did they.
>
> And it came to pass, that at midnight the Lord smote all the firstborn in the land of Egypt, from the firstborn of Pharaoh that sat on his throne unto the firstborn of the captive that was in the dungeon; and all the firstborn of cattle. And Pharaoh rose up in the night, he, and all his servants, and all the Egyptians; and there was a great cry in Egypt; for there was not a house where there was not one dead. And he called for Moses and Aaron by night, and said, Rise up, and get you forth from among my people, both ye and the children of Israel; and go, serve the Lord, as ye have said. Also take your flocks and your herds, as ye have said, and be gone; and bless me also (Exo. 11:1–12:32).

Let us consider Moses' words to the people, especially the phrase "shall not a dog move his tongue."

> But against any of the children of Israel shall not a dog move his tongue, against man or beast: that ye may know how that the Lord doth put a difference between the Egyptians and Israe"

All the Types and Shadows of the Old Testament

(11:7).

That numerous opinions envelop this phrase is true which makes it difficult to determine and ascertain the meaning attached to it. Some, such as Albert Barnes, have suggested the phrase is but a proverb.[2]

Jamison, Fausset and Brown contend:

> No town or village in Egypt or in the East generally is free from the nuisance of dogs, who prowl about the streets and make the most hideous noise at any passers-by at night. What an emphatic significance does the knowledge of this circumstance give to this fact in the sacred record, that on the awful night that was coming, when the air should be rent with the piercing shrieks of mourners, so great and universal would be the panic inspired by the hand of God, that not a dog would move his tongue against the children of Israel! (sic)[3]

Keil and Delitzsch are of the persuasion:

> Moses' address to Pharaoh forms the continuation of his brief answer in Exo 10:29. At midnight Jehovah would go out through the midst of Egypt. This midnight could not be "the one following the day on which Moses was summoned to Pharaoh after the darkness," as Baumgarten supposes; for it was not till after this conversation with the king that Moses received the divine directions as to the Passover, and they must have been communicated to the people at least four days before the feast of the Passover and their departure from Egypt (Exo. 12:3). What

---

[2] Albert Barnes
[3] Jamison, Fausset and Brown

Israelite Homes During the Death of the Firstborn

midnight is meant, cannot be determined. So much is certain, however, that the last decisive blow did not take place in the night following the cessation of the ninth plague; but the institution of the Passover, the directions of Moses to the people respecting the things which they were to ask for from the Egyptians, and the preparations for the feast of the Passover and the exodus, all came between. The "going out" of Jehovah from His heavenly seat denotes His direct inter-position in, and judicial action upon, the world of men. The last blow upon Pharaoh was to be carried out by Jehovah Himself, whereas the other plagues had been brought by Moses and Aaron.

מִצְרַיִם בְּתוֹךְ "**in (through) the midst of Egypt**:" the judgment of God would pass from the centre of the kingdom, the king's throne, over the whole land. "Every first-born shall die, from the first-born of Pharaoh, that sitteth upon his throne, even unto the first-born of the maid that is behind the mill," i.e., the meanest slave (cf. Exo. 12:29, where the captive in the dungeon is substituted for the maid, prisoners being often employed in this hard labour (Jdg. 16:21; Isa. 47:2), "and all the first-born of cattle." This stroke was to fall upon both man and beast as a punishment for Pharaoh's conduct in detaining the Israelite and their cattle; but only upon the first-born, for God did not wish to destroy the Egyptians and their cattle altogether, but simply to show them that He had the power to do this. The first-born represented the whole race, of which it was the strength and bloom (Gen. 49:3). But against the whole of the people of Israel "not a dog shall point its tongue" (Exo. 11:7). The dog points its tongue to growl and bite. The thought expressed in this proverb, which occurs again in Jos. 10:21 and Judith 11:19, was that Israel

All the Types and Shadows of the Old Testament

would not suffer the slightest injury, either in the case of "man or beast." By this complete preservation, whilst Egypt was given up to death, Israel would discover that Jehovah had completed the separation between them and the Egyptians. The effect of this stroke upon the Egyptians would be "a great cry," having no parallel before or after (cf. Exo. 10:14); and the consequence of this cry would be, that the servants of Pharaoh would come to Moses and entreat them to go out with all the people. "At thy feet," i.e., in thy train (vid., Deu. 11:6; Jdg. 8:5). With this announcement Moses departed from Pharaoh in great wrath. Moses' wrath was occasioned by the king's threat (Exo. 10:28), and pointed to the wrath of Jehovah, which Pharaoh would soon experience. As the more than human patience which Moses had displayed towards Pharaoh manifested to him the long-suffering and patience of his God, in whose name and by whose authority he acted, so the wrath of the departing servant of God was to show to the hardened king, that the time of grace was at an end, and the wrath of God was about to burst upon him. (sic emphasis theirs)4

It is well to remind the reader of the background of the text quoted above. The Israelites, who had lived in the land of Egypt for over four hundred years, were well aware of the numerous gods worshiped by the Egyptians).

Every plague God put upon the Egyptians was an assault against the Egyptian gods. When Pharaoh ordered the death of the male children of the Israelites by casting them into the Nile river, his purpose was to have those children offered to the god of the Nile River. The name of the god of the Nile was Hapi. The Egyptians worshiped cows, dogs, frogs and even insects. Thus

Israelite Homes During the Death of the Firstborn

every plague God placed upon the Egyptians was an assault against the gods worshiped by the Egyptians. When the Lord said, through Moses, "... *against any of the children of Israel shall not a dog move his tongue, against man or beast...*" Moses was referring to Anubis, the Egyptian god of the living and dead. Anubis was the god who supposedly escorted the dead to the afterlife and judgment. As Keil and Delitzsch observed regarding the death of the first born, they observe: "The last blow upon Pharaoh was to be carried out by Jehovah Himself, whereas the other plagues had been brought by Moses and Aaron."

Images of the god Anubis

When one examines the Sphinx of Egypt it is clear it is strongly out of portion. The original Sphinx was quite different than that which survives today. The original Sphinx was a monument to Anubis and had the head of a dog as seen in the figures on the next page.

All the Types and Shadows of the Old Testament

The declaration of Exo. 11:7; "*shall not a dog move his tongue, against man or beast: that ye may know how that the Lord doth put a difference between the Egyptians and Israel,*" helps one to rightly understand the purpose and magnitude of the passage. Anubis was unable to prevent the death of the first born of the Egyptians of either man or beast, nor could Anubis take the life of any Israelite.

Understanding the purpose and magnitude of Exo. 11:7 also provides the Bible student with a better knowledge and understanding of the death of the firstborn and also

Israelite Homes During the Death of the Firstborn

serves one well with a better understanding the event of the passing over of the houses of the Israelites by the destroyer as recorded in Exo. 12:23. Israel was considered by the Lord as His firstborn: "*And thou shalt say unto Pharaoh, Thus saith the Lord, Israel is my son, even my firstborn*" (Exo. 4:22). While all the firstborn of man and beasts in Egypt were smitten by the destroyer, none were smitten in the houses of the Israelites.

Now the importance of the houses of the Israelites comes into better focus. The homes of the Israelites represent the church in type in the following ways.

1. Only the Lord's people were in the houses.

Only the Lord's children are in the church.

2. The door posts and header of each house were sealed by the blood of a Passover lamb.

Only the church is sealed by the blood of Christ, our Passover lamb: "...*For even Christ our Passover is sacrificed for us*..." (I Cor. 5:7). See also Acts 20:28; Eph. 1:7; Col. 1:14.

3. To be saved from the destroyer, one had to remain in the house.

To remain saved from the destroyer today one must remain in the church (I Cor. 15:1-2; Col. 1:23; II Thes. 2:15; II John 8).

4. The Passover meal was to be remembered.

The Lord's supper is a memorial for the Christian (I Cor. 11:20-22, 33).

All the Types and Shadows of the Old Testament

5. The Passover meal was eaten by God's people in their houses.

The memorial of the Lord's supper is for the children of the Lord who are in the house of God, the church (I Tim. 3:15).

6. Only one rule of law regulated the nation of Israel.

Only one rule of law regulates the kingdom of God (Gal. 6:2; Jas. 1:25; 2:12).

7. Only one people of God in many houses.

Only one people of God in many congregations (Rom. 12:4-5; 16:16).

8. Every Israelite was to be fully dressed ready to depart Egypt ready to depart in haste.

Every Christian must be properly dressed, ready to depart from the earth at a moment's notice (Gal. 3:26-27; Matt. 22:11-12; Eph. 6:13-17).

Pharaoh:
A Type of Satan

That Pharaoh was a sinister and menacing character is truly an understatement. One of the many ungodly things Pharaoh expressed to Moses and Aaron was when Pharaoh said, *"Who is the Lord, that I should obey his voice to let Israel go? I know not the Lord, neither will I let Israel go"* (Exo. 5:2). Each Pharaoh, the king of Egypt, was considered as the supreme god of Egypt during their reigns, and were thus were not to be challenged by lesser gods. Pharaoh had no knowledge of the God of Israel and would not bow to, nor subject himself to a god of whom he had no knowledge. This well explains his remark in the passage noted above.

Pharoah was an habitual liar during his discourses with Moses. Pharoah made the following comments to Moses which clearly pictures him as a type of Satan.

1. *"Then Pharaoh called for Moses and Aaron, and said, Entreat the Lord, that he may take away the frogs from me, and from my people; and I will let the people go, that they may do sacrifice unto the Lord"* (Exo. 8:8).

- Here we see Pharaoh having involved himself in the "if you do this, then I will do that" scheme.

Just as Pharaoh never planned to let Israel depart, the Devil always plans to keep his victims in bondage to sin.

- Satan three times directly used the same tactic with Jesus (Matt. 4:1-11; and uses the same tactic with us today, Jas. 1:13-15).

All the Types and Shadows of the Old Testament

2. "*And Pharaoh said, I will let you go, that ye may sacrifice to the Lord your God in the wilderness; only ye shall not go very far away: intreat for me*" (Exo. 8:28).

- Pharaoh attempted to draw in Moses and Aaron with a modified lie, hoping to persuade them to adopt his false offer.

Satan operates in the same fashion. Satan wants none of his captives to venture far from him and turn to the Lord. Every soul saved by the Lord is a soul the Devil loses. Every soul the Lord loses is one captured by the Devil.

3. "*Intreat the Lord (for it is enough) that there be no more mighty thunderings and hail; and I will let you go, and ye shall stay no longer*" (Exo. 9:28).

- Pharaoh altered his falsehood in this effort, never intending to honor his own decree.

Satan follows the same pattern, never intending to allow anyone in his trap escape (I Peter 1:8).

4. "*And Moses and Aaron were brought again unto Pharaoh: and he said unto them, Go, serve the Lord your God: but who are they that shall go? And Moses said, We will go with our young and with our old, with our sons and with our daughters, with our flocks and with our herds will we go; for we must hold a feast unto the Lord. And he said unto them, Let the Lord be so with you, as I will let you go, and your little ones: look to it; for evil is before you. Not so: go now ye that are men, and serve the Lord; for that ye did desire. And they were driven out from Pharaoh's presence*" (Exo. 10:8–11).

- Pharaoh modified his false narrative with the word "but." You can go, "but."

Satan does all he can to cause men to leave something

Pharaoh: A Type of Satan

with him in order to entice them to return to him (I Pet. 4:1-4).

5. "And Pharaoh called unto Moses, and said, Go ye, serve the Lord; only let your flocks and your herds be stayed: let your little ones also go with you" (Exo. 10:24).
- Here we have the same scheme as mentioned above, but with trickery added.

When the Devil sees one of his damnable efforts fail, he fabricates a new one in hopes of regaining the soul he lost to the Lord (Gal. 1:6-9).

6. Pharaoh was the ruler of a people held in physical captivity.

Satan is the ruler of people held in spiritual captivity (II Cor 4:4).

7. Pharaoh inflicted his captives with hard rigor.

Satan inflicts his captives with sinful rigor.

8. Pharaoh opposed God in everything.

Satan opposes God in everything.

9. Pharaoh used his servants to execute much punishment upon God's people.

Satan uses his serving angels to cause punishment upon God's people (II Cor 11:12-15; 12:7).

10. Pharaoh sought to destroy God's people.

Satan seeks to destroy God's children (I Pet. 5:8).

Five times Pharaoh said he would let Israel depart from Egypt and five times he hardened his heart and lied.

All the Types and Shadows of the Old Testament

Pharaoh was Satan in type. His conversations with Moses were filled with lies and should remind the reader of the words of Christ when he spake of the Devil:

> *Ye are of your father the devil, and the lusts of your father ye will do. He was a murderer from the beginning, and abode not in the truth, because there is no truth in him. When he speaketh a lie, he speaketh of his own: for <u>he is a liar, and the father of it</u> (John 8:44).*

The Passover Lamb: A Type of Christ

John called Jesus *"the Lamb of God,"* which clearly establishes Him as our Passover Lamb (John 1:29, 36; I Cor. 5:7; Rev. 5:12).

Jesus was crucified during Passover, and as a Jew He was required to go to Jerusalem to celebrate it. Jesus did not just happen to die during Passover. In I Cor. 5:7; Paul said plainly:

> *"Purge out therefore the old leaven, that ye may be a new lump, as ye are unleavened. For even <u>Christ our passover</u> is sacrificed for us."*

This was not by accident, nor a coincidence. Jesus was crucified during the time of the Passover in order to fulfill the type of the Passover Lamb in Himself.

1. The Passover Lamb had to be eaten exactly as God commanded (Exo. 12:8–11).

Saints must partake of Jesus' body and blood (the Lord's Supper) as He commanded (I Cor. 11:20-34).

2. The blood of the Passover Lamb saved the obedient (Exo. 12:12-13).

The blood of Christ, our Passover Lamb, saves those obedient to Him, Acts 20:28; Rev. 1:5; I Pet. 1:18-19).

3. The Passover Lamb was to be without spot or blemish (Exo. 12:5).

Christ, our Passover Lamb was without spot or blemish

All the Types and Shadows of the Old Testament

(I Pet. 1:19).

4. No bones of the Passover Lamb were to be broken. Exo. 12:46; Num. 9:12.

No bones of Christ were broken during His crucifixion (Psa. 34:20; John 19:33-36).

5. The Passover Lamb was to be eaten on a specific day (Exo. 12:6–8).

The Lord's Supper is to be consumed on a specific day (Acts 20:7).

6. The Israelites had to eat of Passover Lamb properly dressed (Exo. 20:11).

Saints are to examine themselves and be properly dressed when partaking of the Lord's Supper (I Cor. 11:26-29; II Cor. 13:5; Eph. 6:11–18).

7. The Israelites had to eat the Passover Lamb in haste, ready to depart Egypt, leaving things of Egyptian worship and their gods behind.

Saints must leave the things of the world behind, and partake of the Lord's Supper well-prepared to depart this life (I Cor. 11:20-34).

Many of the Israelites disobeyed the Lord when they left Egypt. Both Ezekiel and Amos make mention of this disobedience; as well as Stephen.

> "Wilt thou judge them, son of man, wilt thou judge them? cause them to know the abominations of their fathers: And say unto them, Thus saith the Lord God; In the day when I chose Israel, and lifted up mine hand unto the seed of the house of Jacob, and made myself known unto them in the land of Egypt, when I lifted up mine

The Passover Lamb: A Type of Christ

> hand unto them, saying, I am the Lord your God; In the day that I lifted up mine hand unto them, to bring them forth of the land of Egypt into a land that I had espied for them, flowing with milk and honey, which is the glory of all lands: Then said I unto them, Cast ye away every man the abominations of his eyes, and defile not yourselves with the idols of Egypt: I am the Lord your God. But they rebelled against me, and would not hearken unto me: they did not every man cast away the abominations of their eyes, neither did they forsake the idols of Egypt: then I said, I will pour out my fury upon them, to accomplish my anger against them in the midst of the land of Egypt. But I wrought for my name's sake, that it should not be polluted before the heathen, among whom they were, in whose sight I made myself known unto them, in bringing them forth out of the land of Egypt. Wherefore I caused them to go forth out of the land of Egypt, and brought them into the wilderness" (Eze. 20:4–10).

Notice specifically verse 8 again:

> "But they rebelled against me, and would not hearken unto me: they did not every man cast away the abominations of their eyes, neither did they forsake the idols of Egypt: then I said, I will pour out my fury upon them, to accomplish my anger against them in the midst of the land of Egypt."

The prophet Amos also noted this disobedience of the Israelites when they departed Egypt, saying:

> "But ye have borne the tabernacle of your Moloch and Chiun your images, the star of your god, which ye made to yourselves. Therefore will I cause you to go into captivity beyond Damascus, saith the Lord, whose name is The God of hosts" (Amos 5:26-27).

All the Types and Shadows of the Old Testament

Stephen said:

> *"Yea, ye took up the tabernacle of Moloch, and the star of your god Remphan, figures which ye made to worship them: and I will carry you away beyond Babylon" (Acts 7:43).*

Crossing the Red Sea: A Type of Baptism

When considering the crossing of the Red Sea, it is well to delve deeply into the history of the Israelites during their time in Egypt and in the wilderness. Much is to be considered concerning the crossing of the Red Sea and what it portrays as a type of New Testament baptism.

That the crossing of the Red Sea by the Israelite serves as a type of New Testament baptism was plainly stated by the apostle Paul:

> *Moreover, brethren, I would not that ye should be ignorant, how that all our fathers were under the cloud, and all passed through the sea; And were all baptized unto Moses in the cloud and in the sea (I Cor. 10:1-2).*

A more explicit statement could not have been made. This shows the importance of the pictures of the Old Testament for one to notice as one studies the New Testament.

There are at least ten matters to consider regarding the crossing of the Red Sea by the Israelites, which shall be addressed later. It is interesting to also observe the Israelites were not identified as Jews until after they left Egypt and crossed the Red Sea. Not a few Bible scholars have suggested the word Jew means; "*worshipper of God*".

While in Egypt many of the Israelites were addicted to the worship of many of the gods worshipped by the

All the Types and Shadows of the Old Testament

Egyptians. At least two tabernacles of the gods worshipped by the Egyptians were carried out of Egypt by a number of the Israelites (Amos 5:25-27).

However, we must suppose the majority of the Israelites worshipped the Lord as instructed by Moses and the Law received at Sinai, but untold is the number of those who remained addicted to the worship of a numerous Egyptian gods as they journeyed in the wilderness.

We do ourselves well to learn of an additional reason, unobserved by most Bible students, which contributed to the death of all the Israelites in the wilderness who departed Egypt.

Consider the following disobedience of the Israelites while they were in the wilderness.

> *And it came to pass, when all the kings of the Amorites, which were on the side of Jordan westward, and all the kings of the Canaanites, which were by the sea, heard that the Lord had dried up the waters of Jordan from before the children of Israel, until we were passed over, that their heart melted, neither was there spirit in them any more, because of the children of Israel.*
>
> *At that time the Lord said unto Joshua, Make thee sharp knives, and circumcise again the children of Israel the second time. And Joshua made him sharp knives, and circumcised the children of Israel at the hill of the foreskins. And this is the cause why Joshua did circumcise: All the people that came out of Egypt, that were males, even all the men of war, died in the wilderness by the way, after they came out of Egypt. Now all the people that came out were circumcised: but all the people that were born in the wilderness by the way as they came forth out of Egypt, them they had not*

Crossing the Red Sea: A Type of Baptism

> *circumcised. For the children of Israel walked forty years in the wilderness, till all the people that were men of war, which came out of Egypt, were consumed, because they obeyed not the voice of the Lord: unto whom the Lord sware that he would not shew them the land, which the Lord sware unto their fathers that he would give us, a land that floweth with milk and honey. And their children, whom he raised up in their stead, them Joshua circumcised: for they were uncircumcised, because they had not circumcised them by the way. And it came to pass, when they had done circumcising all the people, that they abode in their places in the camp, till they were whole. And the Lord said unto Joshua, This day have I rolled away the reproach of Egypt from off you. Wherefore the name of the place is called Gilgal unto this day (Josh. 5:1–9).*

It clear from this passage one of the reasons the Israelites died in the wilderness was because they had not continued practicing circumcision during the time they were in the wilderness. Circumcision was a sign of the covenant God gave to Abraham and was to be kept perpetually. Failing to do so was to break the covenant God made with Abraham as recorded in Genesis seventeen.

> *"And God said unto Abraham, Thou shalt keep my covenant therefore, thou, and thy seed after thee in their generations. This is my covenant, which ye shall keep, between me and you and thy seed after thee; Every man child among you shall be circumcised. And ye shall circumcise the flesh of your foreskin; and it shall be a token of the covenant betwixt me and you. And he that is eight days old shall be circumcised among you, every man child in your generations, he that is born in the house, or bought with money of any stranger, which is not of thy seed. He that is born in thy*

All the Types and Shadows of the Old Testament

> house, and he that is bought with thy money, must needs be circumcised: and my covenant shall be in your flesh for an everlasting covenant. And the uncircumcised man child whose flesh of his foreskin is not circumcised, that soul shall be cut off from his people; he hath broken my covenant" (Gen. 17:9–14)

A third reason the Israelites died in the wilderness is recorded in Amos 5:25-26. Keil and Delitzsch give the following comments on this passage:

> The question, "*Have ye offered me sacrifices?*" is equivalent to a denial, and the words apply to the nation as a whole, or the great mass of the people, individual exceptions being passed by. The forty years are used as a round number, to denote the time during which the people were sentenced to die in the wilderness after the rebellion at Kadesh, just as in Num. 14:33–34, and Josh. 5:6, where this time, which actually amounted to only thirty-eight years, is given, as it is here, as forty years. And "the prophet could speak all the more naturally of forty years, since the germ of apostasy already existed in the great mass of the people, even when they still continued outwardly to maintain their fidelity to the God of Israel" (Hengstenberg). During that time even the circumcision of the children born in the thirty-eight years was suspended (see at Josh. 5:5–7)".4

A third reason the Israelites died in the wilderness was because of their distrust in the Lord and their lack of confidence found in both Joshua and Caleb. Consider the following record of Moses, who wrote:

> Say unto them, As truly as I live, saith the Lord, as ye have spoken in mine ears, so will I do to you:

Crossing the Red Sea: A Type of Baptism

> *Your carcasses shall fall in this wilderness; and all that were numbered of you, according to your whole number, from twenty years old and upward, which have murmured against me. Doubtless ye shall not come into the land, concerning which I sware to make you dwell therein, save Caleb the son of Jephunneh, and Joshua the son of Nun. But your little ones, which ye said should be a prey, them will I bring in, and they shall know the land which ye have despised. But as for you, your carcasses, they shall fall in this wilderness. And your children shall wander in the wilderness forty years, and bear your whoredoms, until your carcasses be wasted in the wilderness (Num. 14:28–33).*

So why did the Lord grant the Israelites forty years in the wilderness before destroying them? Such is because He gave the people time to repent.

We recall the Lord said:

> *For I will pass through the land of Egypt this night, and will smite all the firstborn in the land of Egypt, both man and beast; and against all the gods of Egypt I will execute judgment: I am the Lord (Exo. 12:12).*

Earlier we noted many of the Israelites carried the tabernacles of both Molech and Chuin with then out of Egypt and into the wilderness, as stated in Amos 5:25-27 and Acts 7:43. For three reasons God caused the Israelites to die in the wilderness. *First*, because of their not having been circumcised during their time in Egypt, violating the covenant God gave to Abraham. *"And the uncircumcised man child whose flesh of his foreskin is not circumcised, that soul shall be cut off from his people; he hath broken my covenant"* (Gen. 17:14).

A *second* reason the Israelites died in the wilderness is

All the Types and Shadows of the Old Testament

because they carried the tabernacles of Molech and Chiun with them out of Egypt and involved themselves in the worship thereof (Amos 5:25-27; Acts 7:43).

The *third* reason they died in the wilderness is because of their distrust in the Lord in contrast to the confidence shown by both Joshua and Caleb.

Now concerning the event of the crossing of the Red Sea and how it serves as a type of baptism, observe the following.

1. The baptism of the Israelites unto Moses allowed them to leave bondage of their oppressor.

Men leave the bondage of Satan when they are baptized into Christ (Rom. 6:3-4).

2. The Israelites were buried in "baptism unto Moses," I Cor. 10:1–2.

Saints are baptized into Christ (Gal. 3:26-27; Rom. 6:3-4).

3. After their "baptism unto Moses," the Israelites were no longer slaves in Egypt (Exo. 14:22, 28).

Saints are no longer slaves to sin when they are baptized (Rom 6:6).

4. After the Israelites were "baptized into Moses" they were given a new Law by which to live under the dominion of God (Exo.–Deut.).

When one is baptized into Christ he is given a new Law by which to live under the dominion of God (Jer. 31:31; Heb. 8:6–10).

Crossing the Red Sea: A Type of Baptism

5. Everyone "baptized into Moses" was rescued from the bondage of Egypt (Exo. 14:30).

Everyone "baptized into Christ" is rescued from the bondage of sin (Acts 22:16).

6. The Israelites left an old life and began a new one (Exo. 14:13-14).

When one is baptized unto Christ he leaves the old life of sin and begins a new life (Rom. 6:3-11; II Cor. 5:17; Gal. 6:15).

7. The Israelites began to serve a new law giver, Moses (Exo.–Deut.).

Those baptized into Christ serve a new Law giver (Heb. 8:6-10; 9:15).

8. The Israelites baptized unto Moses began a new life (Exo. 14:13–31).

Those baptized into Christ begin a new life (Rom. 6:4; Col. 3:1).

9. The baptism of the Israelites paved their way to the land of promise (Exo. 14:13).

Those baptized into Christ have their way paved for their land of promise (Heb. 7:19; 11:40).

10. The Israelites who were baptized unto Moses left a life of bondage.

Those baptized into Christ gain a life of liberty (Gal. 5:1–13).

11. The Israelites were simply called a "people" (Exo. 1:9, 20; 3:7, 10, 12, etc.) until they were "baptized unto

All the Types and Shadows of the Old Testament

Moses," after which they were called a "nation" or "kingdom" (Exo. 19:6; 33:13; Lev. 18:26).

It isn't until we are "baptized into Christ" that we become part of His kingdom, His royal nation (I Pet.2:9; Col.1:13).

Manna from Heaven: A Type of Christ

The manna provided by God for Israel in the wilderness serves as a type of Christ. The following considers ways in which the manna God sent from heaven is yet another portrait of Christ.

After the Israelites departed Egypt and crossed the Red Sea they murmured against Moses and Aaron for the lack of food. God, however, gave them Manna from heaven to test their willingness to obey Him.

> *Then said the Lord unto Moses, Behold, I will rain bread from heaven for you; and the people shall go out and gather a certain rate every day, that I may prove them, whether they will walk in my law, or no (Exo. 16:4).*

God instructed the Israelites gather a daily portion according to their households. On the sixth day they were gather twice as much to in order to provide them with food on the Sabbath Day.

> *And it shall come to pass, that on the sixth day they shall prepare that which they bring in; and it shall be twice as much as they gather daily (Exo. 16:5).*

The Israelites were to gather their portions of manna daily and not procrastinate, leaving the gathering of it for the following day.

> *This is the thing which the Lord hath commanded, Gather of it every man according to his*

All the Types and Shadows of the Old Testament

> *eating, an omer for every man, according to the number of your persons; take ye every man for them which are in his tents.*
>
> *And the children of Israel did so, and gathered, some more, some less. And when they did mete it with an omer, he that gathered much had nothing over, and he that gathered little had no lack; they gathered every man according to his eating.*
>
> *And Moses said, Let no man leave of it till the morning. Notwithstanding they hearkened not unto Moses; but some of them left of it until the morning, and it bred worms, and stank: and Moses was wroth with them. And they gathered it every morning, every man according to his eating: and when the sun waxed hot, it melted (Exo. 16:16–21).*

The manna God provided was to sustain them during their time in the wilderness. The provision of manna, however, ceased.

> *And the children of Israel did eat manna forty years, until they came to a land inhabited; they did eat manna, until they came unto the borders of the land of Canaan (Exo. 16:35).*

1. God gave the children of Israel manna to prove their obedience to Him (Exo. 16:4).

God gave His Son as the bread of life to prove men today (John 6:48–71).

2. The manna was a temporary blessing (Exo. 16:35).

The manna of Christ is eternal (John 6:50).

3. God gave Israel manna by His grace (Exo. 16:11–30).

Christ was given by God's grace for all men (Heb. 2:9).

Manna from Heaven: A Type of Christ

4. Manna came from heaven (Exo. 16:4; Neh. 9:15).
Christ came from heaven (John 6:38, 62).

5. The manna was sweet as honey (Exo. 16:31).
Christ's words are sweet and precious (Heb. 6:5).

6. Manna was given to Israel by God's divine promise (Exo. 16:4).
Christ was given by God's promise (Isa. 7:14).

7. Manna had to be gathered and prepared (Exo. 16:16–23).
Men must prepare themselves for eternity with the bread of life (John 14:15; 15:14; Eph. 6:24).

8. All manna stored and left uneaten spoiled (Exo. 16:10, 20).
Those who refuse to eat of Christ, the bread of life, will be spoiled eternally (Heb. 10:29–31).

9. The manna ceased once the Israelites reached the promised land (Exo. 16:35; Jos. 5:10–12).
Once saints reach heaven they will eat of the tree of life (Rev. 22:14).

10. The manna was given only to the Israelites (Exo. 16:6-9; John 6:31–49).
Christ was given for the whole world John 3:16; Rom. 5:8–10.

All the Types and Shadows of the Old Testament

The Smitten Rock: A Type of Christ

Inspiration could not have painted a clearer picture pointing to Christ than through the smitten rock as recorded in Exodus 17.

> And all the congregation of the children of Israel journeyed from the wilderness of Sin, after their journeys, according to the commandment of the Lord, and pitched in Rephidim.
>
> And there was no water for the people to drink. Wherefore the people did chide with Moses, and said, Give us water that we may drink.
>
> And Moses said unto them, Why chide ye with me? wherefore do ye tempt the Lord?
>
> And the people thirsted there for water; and the people murmured against Moses, and said, Wherefore is this that thou hast brought us up out of Egypt, to kill us and our children and our cattle with thirst?
>
> And Moses cried unto the Lord, saying, What shall I do unto this people? they be almost ready to stone me.
>
> And the Lord said unto Moses, Go on before the people, and take with thee of the elders of Israel; and thy rod, wherewith thou smotest the river, take in thine hand, and go. Behold, I will stand before thee there upon the rock in Horeb; and thou shalt smite the rock, and there shall come water out of it, that the people may drink.

All the Types and Shadows of the Old Testament

> *And Moses did so in the sight of the elders of Israel. And he called the name of the place Massah, and Meribah, because of the chiding of the children of Israel, and because they tempted the Lord, saying, Is the Lord among us, or not (Exo. 17:1–7).*

The apostle Paul said: "And did all drink the same spiritual drink: for they drank of that spiritual Rock that followed them: and that Rock was Christ" (I Cor. 10:4). When any inspired author informs the reader that what occurred in the Old Testament serves as a type in the New Testament, such forever determines the matter. That the smitten rock of Exodus 17 serves as a portrait of Christ should not be contested.

Several things about the historical event of the smitten rock warrant keen observation. Notice the following sterling points which plainly establish Christ as the fruition of the smitten rock of Exodus 17. In both II Samuel 22 and Psalm 89 the Lord is called the rock of salvation. "*The Lord liveth; and blessed be my rock; and exalted be the God of the rock of my salvation*" (II Sam. 22:47). "*He shall cry unto me, Thou art my father, my God, and the rock of my salvation*" (Psa. 89:26).

1. The rock of Exo. 17 was smitten for the benefit of God's people, providing life sustaining water (Exo. 17:5–7).

Christ was smitten for the benefit of mankind who provides obedient men with living water.

> "*Jesus answered and said unto her, If thou knewest the gift of God, and who it is that saith to thee, Give me to drink; thou wouldest have asked of him, and he would have given thee living water*" (John 4:10).

The Smitten Rock: A Type of Christ

"And he said unto me, It is done. I am Alpha and Omega, the beginning and the end. I will give unto him that is athirst of the fountain of the water of life freely" (Rev. 21:6).

2. An abundant flow of water came forth from the smitten rock to supply water for all Israel (Exo. 17:5–7).

Christ is the source of spiritual water (Rev. 21:6; John 4:10; Rev. 22:17).

3. The smitten rock is a symbol of strength and refuge (Psa. 94:22; Isa. 17:10).

Christ is the strength and refuge for those who come to Him (Heb. 5:8-9; Psa. 18:35; 20:6; Luke 22:69; Acts 5:31).

4. The smitten rock was a rock of stability and could not be moved or changed.

Christ is a rock which cannot be moved or changed (Heb. 13:8; Mal. 3:6; Jas. 1:17).

5. The rock was smitten in the presence of all the people (Exo. 17:5-6).

Christ was crucified, smitten publicly (Matt. 27:35–54; John 19:18–22).

6. The water from the smitten rock could not be replaced, for there was no other source from which Israel could acquire water.

The living water of Christ cannot be substituted (John 14:6; Acts 4:12; I Cor. 3:11).

7. The rock had to be smitten before water became available to Israel (Exo. 17:6).

Christ had to be crucified and His blood shed before

All the Types and Shadows of the Old Testament

salvation could be made available (Heb. 9:22; 10:12; I Pet. 1:19).

8. The water from the rock had to be consumed to be beneficial (Exo. 17:5–7).

The life-giving water of Christ must be consumed before man can be saved (Heb. 5:8-9; Rev. 22:14; John 14:6).

9. The smitten rock was that which saved the lives of Israel (Exo. 17:6).

The smitten Christ is the avenue by which man can be saved (John 8:24; Heb. 10:26–29).

10. The Smitten rock provided the presence of the Lord (Exo. 17:6).

Christ, the smitten rock, provides the presence of the Lord (John 1:14; 14:9).

Mount Sinai: A Type of Mount Zion

As David said, "The heavens declare the glory of God; and the firmament sheweth his handywork" (Psa. 19:1), so it is with the Lord having provided man with many portraits of His supreme glory and wisdom, wonderfully stitched in the tapestry of the scheme of redemption. The same is true when considering Mount Sinai and Mount Zion.

It is nothing less than amazing how the hand of God has painted so many things for students to observe regarding the New Testament church. We have thus far observed numerous pictures from the Lord's divine hand and here we shall observe yet another well-framed depiction of matters regarding the New Testament church.

> In the third month, when the children of Israel were gone forth out of the land of Egypt, the same day came they into the wilderness of Sinai. For they were departed from Rephidim, and were come to the desert of Sinai, and had pitched in the wilderness; and there Israel camped before the mount (Exo. 19:1-2).

The entirety of Exodus 19 has numerous figures and adumbrations which merit much close attention from every student of the Lord's Word.

More than a dozen considerations will be examined in this chapter showing Mount Sinai as a type of Mount Zion. We feel it beneficial to provide visual aids showing

All the Types and Shadows of the Old Testament

the student just where each of these two mountains are geographically located. Notice that Mount Zion is in Jerusalem.

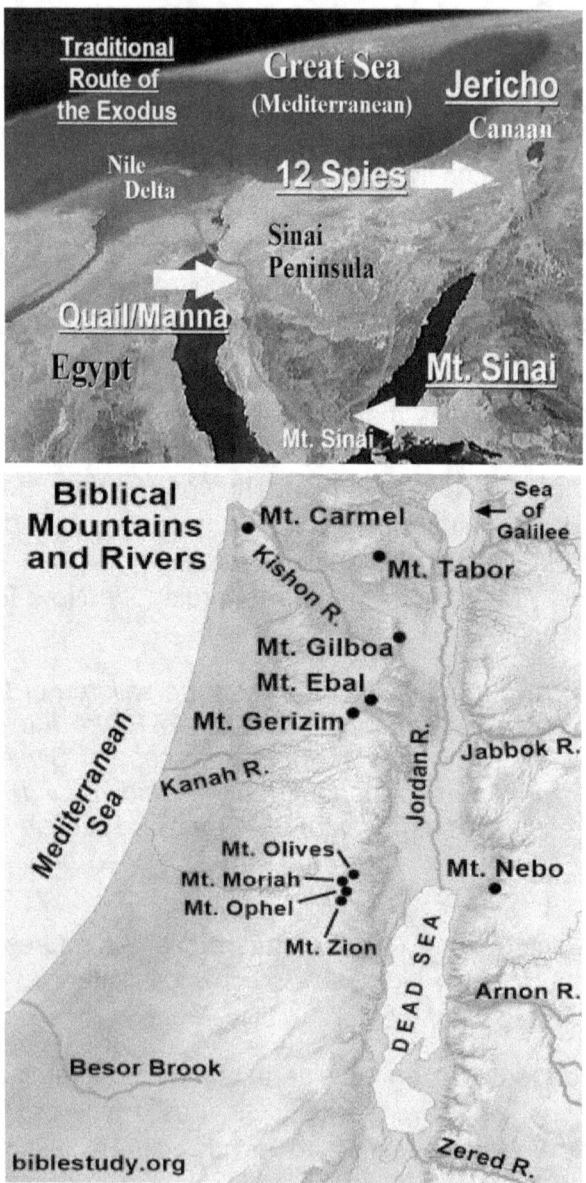

Mount Sinai: A Type of Mount Zion

1. Mount Sinai was covered with a cloud when the Lord spoke to Moses and the people (Exo. 19:9).

Mount Zion was covered with a cloud when the Lord spoke from heaven to Peter (Matt. 17:5).

2. The voice of the Lord was heard from heaven (Exo. 19:9).

The voice of the Lord was heard from heaven (Matt. 17:5).

3. The Old Testament Law was given from the top of Mount Sinai (Exo. 19:3).

The Law of the New Testament was given from the top of Mount Zion (Isa. 2:1–3).

4. The Lord was present on Mount Sinai when the Old Law was given (Exo. 19:1–11).

The Lord was present on Mount Zion from which the New Law was given (Isa. 2:1–3; Matt. 17:1-2).

5. About 3,000 men died physically when the Old Law was given (Exo. 32:28).

About 3,000 men were made spiritually alive when the church was established (Acts 2:41).

6. Mount Sinai could not be touched when the Lord gave the Old Law (Exo. 19:12-13).

Today men are invited to come to Mount Zion (Heb. 12:22).

7. After the Old Law was given from Mount Sinai, the people would become a kingdom of priests (Exo. 19:6).

Those who obey the New Law become part of a holy priesthood (I Pet. 2:5).

All the Types and Shadows of the Old Testament

8. Sanctification was required when the Old Law was given (Exo. 19:10).

Sanctification is required under the New Law (I Cor. 1:30; II Thes. 2:13).

9. Cleanliness was required at Mount Sinai (Exo. 19:14).

Spiritual cleanliness is require by the Law given on Mount Zion (Rev. 3:4).

10. At Mount Sinai the people met with God (Exo. 19:17).

Those of Mount Zion shall meet the Lord (I Thes. 4:17).

11. The Jews had to leave Mount Sinai and journey to a new place (Exo. 33:1).

Christians will leave this world and go to a new Jerusalem and will forever be with the Lord (John 14:1–3; I Thes. 4:13–18).

12. Mount Sinai provided a law of death (II Cor. 3:7).

Mount Zion provides a Law of life (John 6:63; Rom. 8:10).

13. Mount Sinai was chosen by God (Exo. 19:11).

Mount Zion was chosen by God (Isa. 2:2-3; 28:16; Zech. 8:3; Luke 24:47).

14. Moses ascended Mount Sinai and descended it (Exo. 19:3, 20).

Christ descended from heaven to Mount Zion and ascended to it (Acts 1:9–11).

15. Mount Sinai was chosen by God (Exo. 19:3, 20).

Mount Zion was chosen by God (Isa. 2:2-3; Zech. 8:3; Luke 24:47).

Moses' Transfiguration: A Type of Christ's Transfiguration

While there are but a few comparisons and contrasts between Moses' transfigured face and that of the Lord's, there are many matters worthy of consideration regarding Moses' transfiguration. Consider the following passages.

> *And the Lord said unto Moses, Write thou these words: for after the tenor of these words I have made a covenant with thee and with Israel. And he was there with the Lord forty days and forty nights; he did neither eat bread, nor drink water. And he wrote upon the tables the words of the covenant, the ten commandments.*
>
> *And it came to pass, when Moses came down from mount Sinai with the two tables of testimony in Moses' hand, when he came down from the mount, that Moses wist not that the skin of his face shone while he talked with him. And when Aaron and all the children of Israel saw Moses, behold, the skin of his face shone; and they were afraid to come nigh him. And Moses called unto them; and Aaron and all the rulers of the congregation returned unto him: and Moses talked with them. And afterward all the children of Israel came nigh: and he gave them in commandment all that the Lord had spoken with him in mount Sinai. And till Moses had done speaking with them, he put a vail on his face. But when Moses went in before the Lord to speak with him, he took the vail off, until he*

All the Types and Shadows of the Old Testament

came out. And he came out, and spake unto the children of Israel that which he was commanded. And the children of Israel saw the face of Moses, that the skin of Moses' face shone: and Moses put the vail upon his face again, until he went in to speak with him (Exo. 34:27–34).

There are three passages of Scripture which aid the student when considering the phrase "the skin of his face shone" (Exo. 34:30). First for consideration are the words of Paul, who wrote: "*For Christ is the end of the law for righteousness to every one that believeth*" (Rom. 10:4). The phrase "*the end of the law*" literally means Christ was the sole purpose of the Law of Moses. The whole purpose of the Old Law was to bring Christ and His gospel to fruition.

Secondly, Paul declared:

> *But if the ministration of death, written and engraven in stones, was glorious, so that the children of Israel could not stedfastly behold the face of Moses for the glory of his countenance; which glory was to be done away: How shall not the ministration of the spirit be rather glorious? For if the ministration of condemnation be glory, much more doth the ministration of righteousness exceed in glory. For even that which was made glorious had no glory in this respect, by reason of the glory that excelleth. For if that which is done away was glorious, much more that which remaineth is glorious. Seeing then that we have such hope, we use great plainness of speech: And not as Moses, which put a vail over his face, that the children of Israel could not stedfastly look to the end of that which is abolished*" (II Cor. 3:7–13).

We are plainly told by Paul just why Moses' face was veiled after his decent from Mount Sinai. "*Moses, which*

Moses' Transfiguration and Jesus' Transfiguration

put a vail over his face, that the children of Israel could not stedfastly look to the end of that which is abolished" (II Cor. 3:13). The Law of Moses was to come to an end at the time God determined. The Israelites could not look at the end of the Law of Moses, they wished not for it to come to an end, but such was the Lord's intent and plan.

We have inspiration's divine commentary as to why Moses veiled his face when he spoke to Israel once he came down from Mount Sinai. There can be no other conclusion one may properly derive.

Third, one must consider what Paul stated in his epistle to the Galatians.

> *Wherefore then serveth the law? It was added because of transgressions, till the seed should come to whom the promise was made; and it was ordained by angels in the hand of a mediator. Now a mediator is not a mediator of one, but God is one. Is the law then against the promises of God? God forbid: for if there had been a law given which could have given life, verily righteousness should have been by the law. But the scripture hath concluded all under sin, that the promise by faith of Jesus Christ might be given to them that believe. But before faith came, we were kept under the law, shut up unto the faith which should afterwards be revealed. Wherefore the law was our schoolmaster to bring us unto Christ, that we might be justified by faith. But after that faith is come, we are no longer under a schoolmaster. For ye are all the children of God by faith in Christ Jesus (Gal. 3:19–25).*

Here we are given additional divine commentary concerning the purpose of the Law of Moses. The Jews were informed *"the law was our schoolmaster to bring*

All the Types and Shadows of the Old Testament

us unto Christ, that we might be justified by faith" (Gal. 3:25). Indeed the end of the Law of Moses—that is the purpose for ending the Law of Moses—was to escort the Jews to Christ. They would no longer be justified by the Law of Moses, but would have to acquire justification through the system of faith established by Christ.

Moses plainly told the Israelites the time would come when they must give up the Law of Moses and go to Christ. Observe:

> *The Lord thy God will raise up unto thee a Prophet from the midst of thee, of thy brethren, like unto me; unto him ye shall hearken; According to all that thou desiredst of the Lord thy God in Horeb in the day of the assembly, saying, Let me not hear again the voice of the Lord my God, neither let me see this great fire any more, that I die not. And the Lord said unto me, They have well spoken that which they have spoken. I will raise them up a Prophet from among their brethren, like unto thee, and will put my words in his mouth; and he shall speak unto them all that I shall command him. And it shall come to pass, that whosoever will not hearken unto my words which he shall speak in my name, I will require it of him (Deut. 18:15–18).*

It was unto Christ the Israelites were to hearken and submit once He came and fulfilled the time God declared.

> *But when the fulness of the time was come, God sent forth his Son, made of a woman, made under the law, To redeem them that were under the law, that we might receive the adoption of sons. And because ye are sons, God hath sent forth the Spirit of his Son into your hearts, crying,*

Moses' Transfiguration and Jesus' Transfiguration

Abba, Father. Wherefore thou art no more a servant, but a son; and if a son, then an heir of God through Christ (Gal. 4:4–7).

That the purpose for which the Law of Moses was given has been set before the reader should be clear. Inspiration declared the veil which was placed upon Moses' face was symbolic of the ending of the Old Law. Therefore, *"the children of Israel could not stedfastly look to the end of that which is abolished"* (II Cor. 3:13).

1. Moses' face shone at the bottom of Mount Sinai to show it must end (Exo. 34:29).

Christ's face shone on top of Mount Zion to show it was to endure forever (Matt. 17:1-2, 5).

2. The brightness of Moses' face eventually faded (Exo. 34:29–35).

Christ's face remained bright all the while He was on Mount Zion, Matt.:17:1–13.

3. Moses spoke God's Law to the people (Exo. 34:31–33).

Jesus spoke God's new law to the people (John 13:34; Isa. 2:2–4; Heb. 1:1-2).

4. Moses' law was a temporary one (II Cor. 3:7; Heb 8:8-13).

The Lord's law is permanent (II Sam 7:12–17; Dan. 2:44; Luke 1:32-33).

5. Moses' face was veiled in life (Exo. 34:33).

Jesus face was veiled in death (Luke 24:15-16; John 20:7).

All the Types and Shadows of the Old Testament

The Intercession of Moses for the People: A Type of Christ Interceding for the Saints

The intercession of Moses on behalf of the Israelites is a subject which merits much attention from every good Bible student. Proper consideration of this event requires a good accounting of the background preceding this event. We do so here.

That Moses was instructed by the Lord to go to the top of Mount Sinai is not contested by men of faith, who believe and accept that which is recorded in the inspired text. Five passages in Exodus plainly state Moses was to ascend Mount Sanai. We are told: *"And Moses alone shall come near the Lord: but they shall not come nigh; neither shall the people go up with him"* (Exo. 24:2). *"And the Lord said unto Moses, Come up to me into the mount, and be there: and I will give thee tables of stone, and a law, and commandments which I have written; that thou mayest teach them"* (Exo. 24:12). *"And Moses went into the midst of the cloud, and gat him up into the mount: and Moses was in the mount forty days and forty nights"* (Exo. 24:18).

Many insist Moses was atop the mountain alone. However, we have inspired information that Moses was not alone on Mount Sinai during the time he received the Law from the Lord.

Consider the following passage:

> *And Moses rose up, and his minister Joshua:*

All the Types and Shadows of the Old Testament

> *and Moses went up into the mount of God. And he said unto the elders, Tarry ye here for us, until we come again unto you: and, behold, Aaron and Hur are with you: if any man have any matters to do, let him come unto them (Exo. 24:13-14).*

Moses plainly said to the people: "*Tarry ye here for us, until we come again unto you*" (Exo. 24:15). How far up Mount Sinai Joshua ascended, we are not told. But Moses and Joshua did in fact ascend the mount together to a place where Joshua was to remain during Moses' time on the top of Mount Sinai. Moses was no doubt given such instructions by the Lord before their ascent, and both Moses and Joshua obeyed the Lord's commands and journeyed together to the place appointed by the Lord.

Some have speculated that Joshua, like Moses, fasted the forty days during his time on Mount Sinai. This is, however, merely an assumption—inspiration has not affirmed such a position. We might rightfully speculate here that Joshua was granted partial access to Mount Sinai for the purpose of preparing the people to accept him as Moses' replacement once Moses died, but we shall not press the thought.

As Moses began his descent from Mount Sinai, he rejoined Joshua and they continued their journey toward the camp of the Israelites. As Moses and Joshua continued their descent "*Joshua heard the noise of the people as they shouted,*" and he said to Moses, "*There is a noise of war in the camp*" (Exo. 32:17). Moses, however, knew such was not the case, for the "*Lord said unto Moses, Go, get thee down; for thy people, which thou broughtest out of the land of Egypt, have corrupted themselves: They have turned aside quickly out of the way which I commanded them: they have made them a*

Moses' Intercession and Jesus' Intercession

molten calf, and have worshipped it, and have sacrificed thereunto, and said, These be thy gods, O Israel, which have brought thee up out of the land of Egypt" (Exo. 32:7-8).

The inspired record states:

> *And when Joshua heard the noise of the people as they shouted, he said unto Moses, There is a noise of war in the camp. And he [Moses] said, It is not the voice of them that shout for mastery, neither is it the voice of them that cry for being overcome: but the noise of them that sing do I hear. And it came to pass, as soon as he came nigh unto the camp, that he saw the calf, and the dancing: and Moses' anger waxed hot, and he cast the tables out of his hands, and brake them beneath the mount" (Exo. 32:17–19).*

The background now having been set, we turn to the intercession Moses on behalf of Israel. Observe:

> *And the Lord said unto Moses, Go, get thee down; for thy people, which thou broughtest out of the land of Egypt, have corrupted themselves: They have turned aside quickly out of the way which I commanded them: they have made them a molten calf, and have worshipped it, and have sacrificed thereunto, and said, These be thy gods, O Israel, which have brought thee up out of the land of Egypt. And the Lord said unto Moses, I have seen this people, and, behold, it is a stiffnecked people: Now therefore let me alone, that my wrath may wax hot against them, and that I may consume them: and I will make of thee a great nation (Exo. 32:7–10).*

The Psalmist wrote saying:

> *Therefore he said that he would destroy them,*

All the Types and Shadows of the Old Testament

> had not Moses his chosen stood before him in the breach, to turn away his wrath, lest he should destroy them (Psa. 106:23).

Moses began his intercession on behalf of Israel as shown in the following passage:

> *And Moses besought the Lord his God, and said, Lord, why doth thy wrath wax hot against thy people, which thou hast brought forth out of the land of Egypt with great power, and with a mighty hand? Wherefore should the Egyptians speak, and say, For mischief did he bring them out, to slay them in the mountains, and to consume them from the face of the earth? Turn from thy fierce wrath, and repent of this evil against thy people. Remember Abraham, Isaac, and Israel, thy servants, to whom thou swarest by thine own self, and saidst unto them, I will multiply your seed as the stars of heaven, and all this land that I have spoken of will I give unto your seed, and they shall inherit it for ever (Exo. 32:11–13).*

Moses' intercessory prayer for Israel was answered favorably by the Lord. "*And the Lord repented of the evil which he thought to do unto his people*" (Exo. 32:14). We are here compelled to offer commentary regarding the phrase "*the Lord repented.*" When man repents, he changes his will. However, when the Lord repents, He wills a change.

God willed a change of His intent to "*consume them*" and make of Moses a "*great nation*" (Exo. 32 10).

1. It is well to observe the intercessory prayer of Moses on behalf of Israel was expressed while Moses was in the presence of God (Exo. 32:11–13).

Christ, in the presence of God, intercedes for the saints in heaven.

Moses' Intercession and Jesus' Intercession

Therefore will I divide him a portion with the great, and he shall divide the spoil with the strong; because he hath poured out his soul unto death: and he was numbered with the transgressors; and he bare the sin of many, and made intercession for the transgressors (Isa. 53:12).

And he that searcheth the hearts knoweth what is the mind of the Spirit, because he [Christ] maketh intercession for the saints according to the will of God (Rom. 8:27).

Who is he that condemneth? It is Christ that died, yea rather, that is risen again, who is even at the right hand of God, who also maketh intercession for us (Rom. 8:34).

God hath not cast away his people which he foreknew. Wot ye not what the scripture saith of Elias? how he maketh intercession to God against Israel... (Rom. 11:2).

Wherefore he is able also to save them to the uttermost that come unto God by him, seeing he ever liveth to make intercession for them (Heb. 7:25).

2. Moses interceded for the children of Israel (Exo. 32:11-13).

Christ intercedes for the saints (Rom. 8:34; Heb. 7:25).

3. Moses prayed for the Israelites (Exo. 32:11–13).

Jesus prayed for those who believe (John 17:20).

4. Moses was chosen by the Father to intercede for the people.

Jesus was chosen by the Father to intercede for His people (John 3:16).

All the Types and Shadows of the Old Testament

The Consecration of Aaron: A Type of the Consecration of Christ

Numerous things are worthy of consideration regarding the consecration of Aaron and Christ. Consider the following passages:

> *And thou shalt take the garments, and put upon Aaron the coat, and the robe of the ephod, and the ephod, and the breastplate, and gird him with the curious girdle of the ephod: And thou shalt put the mitre upon his head, and put the holy crown upon the mitre. Then shalt thou take the anointing oil, and pour it upon his head, and anoint him (Exo. 29:5–7)*

> *And he put upon him the coat, and girded him with the girdle, and clothed him with the robe, and put the ephod upon him, and he girded him with the curious girdle of the ephod, and bound it unto him therewith. And he put the breastplate upon him: also he put in the breastplate the Urim and the Thummim. And he put the mitre upon his head; also upon the mitre, even upon his forefront, did he put the golden plate, the holy crown; as the Lord commanded Moses. And Moses took the anointing oil, and anointed the tabernacle and all that was therein, and sanctified them (Lev. 8:7–10).*

Observe the following things concerning the anointing of Aaron and of Christ.

All the Types and Shadows of the Old Testament

1. Aaron was anointed as the Lord's chosen (Exo. 30:30).

Christ was chosen as the Lord's anointed (Matt. 16:15; Mark 8:29; Luke 9:20).

2. Aaron was anointed by Moses (Exo. 40:12–15).

Christ was anointed by the Father (II Sam. 7:12–17; Acts 10:38; Psalm 45:7).

3. Aaron was anointed once, by Moses (Exo. 40:13)

Christ was twice anointed—once by a Mary who anointed His head, and once by another Mary who anointed His feet.

> Now when Jesus was in Bethany, in the house of Simon the leper, There came unto him a woman having an alabaster box of very precious ointment, and poured it on his head, as he sat at meat (Matt. 26:6-7).
>
> And being in Bethany in the house of Simon the leper, as he sat at meat, there came a woman having an alabaster box of ointment of spikenard very precious; and she brake the box, and poured it on his head (Mark 14:3)
>
> And one of the Pharisees desired him that he would eat with him. And he went into the Pharisee's house, and sat down to meat. And, behold, a woman in the city, which was a sinner, when she knew that Jesus sat at meat in the Pharisee's house, brought an alabaster box of ointment, And stood at his feet behind him weeping, and began to wash his feet with tears, and did wipe them with the hairs of her head, and kissed his feet, and anointed them with the ointment (Luke 7:36–38).

- In the Matthew and Mark passages we see Jesus in the house of Simon the leper.

Aaron's Consecration and Christ's Consecration

- In Luke we find Jesus in the house of a Pharisee.
- Matthew and Mark show the event early on in Jesus' ministry.
- Luke's account shows the anointing of Jesus feet toward the end of His ministry. These are *not* the same event, as some have suggested.
- Jesus ministry began with an anointment and ended with an anointment.

4. Once anointed only the High priest entered the Most Holy Place (Lev. 16:11–16).

Once anointed only Christ entered into the heavens (Eph. 4:10; Heb. 4:14; 8:1).

5. The High Priest performed only sacred duties (Lev. 16:1–34).

Christ did only the will of the Father (Luke 2:49; John 4:34; 6:38; 8:29).

6. The High Priest had to offer a sacrifice offered on his behalf and of the people (Lev. 16:1–5).

Christ was the sacrifice offered by the Father for others (Rom. 5:8-9; I Pet. 3:18; I John 4:9-10).

7. Only the High priest could take incense into the Most Holy Place (Lev. 16:1–13).

The incense represents the prayers of the saints (Rev. 5:8; 8:3-4).

- The prayers of the saints are as sweet incense to the Father and only Christ intercedes for His people. *"For there is one God, and one mediator between God and men, the man Christ Jesus"* (I Tim. 2:5).
- *"And another angel came and stood at the altar, having a golden censer; and there was given*

All the Types and Shadows of the Old Testament

> *unto him much incense, that he should offer it with the prayers of all saints upon the golden altar which was before the throne" And the smoke of the incense, which came with the prayers of the saints, ascended up before God out of the angel's hand"* (Rev. 8:3-4)

8. The High Priest made atonement for himself and the people (Exo. 30:10; Lev. 16:34).

Christ makes atonement, not for Himself, but only for the saints (Heb. 7:27; 9:7–14; 10:9-10).

9. The High Priest had sole charge of the Tabernacle (Heb. 9:6-7).

Christ has sole authority in the Lord's church (Matt. 28:18; I Cor. 15:24; Eph. 1:22; Col. 1:18).

10. The High Priest made authoritative judgments for the people (Matt. 26:57; John 18:13; Acts 4:6).

Christ is the authoritative judge of all men (Acts 10:42; 17:30-31; Rom. 2:16).

11. The High Priest died and had to be replaced (Heb. 7:23).

Christ forever remains alive as our High priest (Heb. 7:24, 28).

12. The High Priest was to be without blemish (Lev. 21:17–21).

Christ was without spiritual blemish (Heb. 4:15; 7:26; I Pet. 2:22; II Cor. 5:21).

The Levites: A Type of Christians

There is no difficulty in understanding the book of Leviticus pertains to the duties of the Levitical priesthood. The word *Leviticus* means *pertaining to the priests*. There are no historical events recorded in the book of Leviticus except for one particular event—Nadab and Abihu offering strange fire before the Lord while drunk.

That both Nadab and Abihu were drunk, which resulted in their offering unauthorized fire to burn the incense required by the Lord, is clearly seen in verse 9.

> *And Nadab and Abihu, the sons of Aaron, took either of them his censer, and put fire therein, and put incense thereon, and offered strange fire before the Lord, which he commanded them not. And there went out fire from the Lord, and devoured them, and they died before the Lord. Then Moses said unto Aaron, This is it that the Lord spake, saying, I will be sanctified in them that come nigh me, and before all the people I will be glorified. And Aaron held his peace. And Moses called Mishael and Elzaphan, the sons of Uzziel the uncle of Aaron, and said unto them, Come near, carry your brethren from before the sanctuary out of the camp. So they went near, and carried them in their coats out of the camp; as Moses had said. And Moses said unto Aaron, and unto Eleazar and unto Ithamar, his sons, Uncover not your heads, neither rend your clothes; lest ye die, and lest wrath come upon all the people: but let your brethren, the whole house of Israel, bewail*

All the Types and Shadows of the Old Testament

the burning which the Lord hath kindled. And ye shall not go out from the door of the tabernacle of the congregation, lest ye die: for the anointing oil of the Lord is upon you. And they did according to the word of Moses. <u>And the Lord spake unto Aaron, saying, Do not drink wine nor strong drink, thou, nor thy sons with thee, when ye go into the tabernacle of the congregation, lest ye die: it shall be a statute for ever throughout your generations</u>: And that ye may put difference between holy and unholy, and between unclean and clean; And that ye may teach the children of Israel all the statutes which the Lord hath spoken unto them by the hand of Moses" (Lev. 10:1–11).

In every passage of inspired Scripture, the use of strong drink—that is, fermented wine—is always condemned by the Lord. Some argue Paul authorized the use of fermented drink when he instructed Timothy to consume *"a little wine,"* as recorded in I Tim. 5:23, which reads: *"Drink no longer water, but use a little wine for thy stomach's sake and thine often infirmities."* However, consider the following things and the context of the passage. First, there is an ellipsis to be considered here. An ellipsis is a figure of speech wherein a thought is understood though not stated. Paul plainly said to Timothy *"Drink no longer water,"* the elliptical thought of this verse is for Timothy to no longer drink water <u>only</u>, but drink a little wine for his physical ailment, whatever it happened to be.

Further, Paul dictated the measure of wine to be consumed by Timothy. He was drink but *a little*, not be involved in routine consumption of strong drink on whatever occasion Timothy wanted. The measure of the wine was restricted, and the purpose thereof was restricted by the apostle. This passage in no way, even

The Levites: A Type of Christians

in the furthest reach, authorizes the consumption of strong drink. As was stated above, so say we now again: "**In every passage of inspired Scripture the use of strong drink—that is fermented wine—is always condemned by the Lord.**"

The Levites served the Lord in the tabernacle and eventually the temple, and were forbidden to consume strong drink. As saints, Christians serve the Lord in the church and are likewise forbidden to consume strong drink.

Ponder the following fifteen parallels between the Levites and the Christian.

1. The Levites were assigned specific responsibilities in their service to the Lord (Exo. 29).

Christians are assinged specific responsibilities in the Lord's church (II Cor. 6:14–7:1).

2. The Levites had to be without blemish or deformity (Lev. 21:16–24).

Christians must keep themselves without spot (Eph. 5:26-27; Jas. 1:27; I Thes. 5:21-22).

3. The Levites were consecrated for the service of the Lord (Exo. 29).

Christians have been converted to serve the Lord (Acts 3:19; Matt. 18:3).

4. The Levites had to contact the blood of sacrifice (Exo. 29:15–21).

Christians contact the blood of Christ, our sacrifice (Acts 20:28; Col. 1:14; Heb. 9:12–14; I Pet. 1:18-19; Rev. 5:9).

All the Types and Shadows of the Old Testament

5. The Levites were to refrain from unholy things (Lev. 21:1–8).

Christians must refrain from and have nothing to do with unholy things, 1 Thes. 5:22.

6. The Levites were to wash in the laver before entering the Holy Place (Exo. 40:7, 12–15).

Christians have been washed in the blood of Christ by baptism (Acts 20:28; 22:16; I Pet. 1:18-19; 3:21; Rev. 1:5).

7. The Levites were required to wear pure white linen garments (Exo. 29:4–9; II Chron. 5:12).

Christians are to be adorned with the armor of God (Eph. 6:10–18; Rev. 19:8).

8. The Levites served the Lord in the tabernacle (Heb. 9:6; Lev. 1:6–11).

Christians serve the Lord in the church (I Pet. 2:5).

9. The Levites offered daily sacrifices (Exo. 29:38–43).

Christians are to offer their bodies as living sacrifices daily (Rom. 12:1-2; Luke 9:23).

10. The Levites were required to keep the candlestick lit (Exo. 40:4, 25).

Christians are required to be lights to the world (Matt. 5:16; Eph. 5:8; I Thes. 5:5).

11. The Levites were to set the table of unleavened showbread and eat it (Lev. 24:5–9).

Christians are to partake of unleaven bread every first day of every week (Acts 20:7; I Cor. 11:17–33).

The Levites: A Type of Christians

12. The Levites burned incense daily, which pictures the prayers of the saints (Exo. 30:7-8; Rev. 8:3-4).
Christians are to pray daily (I Thes. 5:17).

13. The Levites were forbidden to use strong drink (Lev. 10:9-10).
Christians are forbidden to use strong drink (Eph. 5:18).

14. The Levites were commanded to bless the Lord (I Chron. 23:30).
Christians are required to bless the Lord (Heb. 13:15).

15. The Levites were always to remain faithful to the Lord (Num. 18:7).
Christians are to remain faithful throughout life (II Tim. 4:6–8; Rev. 2:10).

All the Types and Shadows of the Old Testament

The Brazen Serpent: A Type of Christ

We now consider the brazen serpent fashioned by Moses as commanded by the Lord. In John 3 Jesus declared He was the fruition of the type, recorded in Numbers 21, of the serpent on the pole erected by Moses. Jesus said to Nicodemus: *"And as Moses lifted up the serpent in the wilderness, even so must the Son of man be lifted up"* (John 3:14). Consider also the words of Jesus:

> *Now is my soul troubled; and what shall I say? Father, save me from this hour: but for this cause came I unto this hour. Father, glorify thy name.*
>
> *Then came there a voice from heaven, saying, I have both glorified it, and will glorify it again.*
>
> *The people therefore, that stood by, and heard it, said that it thundered: others said, An angel spake to him.*
>
> *Jesus answered and said, This voice came not because of me, but for your sakes. Now is the judgment of this world: now shall the prince of this world be cast out. And I, if I be lifted up from the earth, will draw all men unto me. This he said, signifying what death he should die (John 12:27–33).*

Thus it is clear the serpent Moses reared up serves as a type of Christ on the cross.

The account of Moses raising up the serpent in the wilderness is found in Numbers 21. Observe:

All the Types and Shadows of the Old Testament

> *And they journeyed from mount Hor by the way of the Red sea, to compass the land of Edom: and the soul of the people was much discouraged because of the way. And the people spake against God, and against Moses, Wherefore have ye brought us up out of Egypt to die in the wilderness? for there is no bread, neither is there any water; and our soul loatheth this light bread.*
>
> *And the Lord sent fiery serpents among the people, and they bit the people; and much people of Israel died. Therefore the people came to Moses, and said, We have sinned, for we have spoken against the Lord, and against thee; pray unto the Lord, that he take away the serpents from us.*
>
> *And Moses prayed for the people. And the Lord said unto Moses, Make thee a fiery serpent, and set it upon a pole: and it shall come to pass, that every one that is bitten, when he looketh upon it, shall live.*
>
> *And Moses made a serpent of brass, and put it upon a pole, and it came to pass, that if a serpent had bitten any man, when he beheld the serpent of brass, he lived (Num. 21:4–9).*

Because of the peoples rebellion against the Lord and Moses, the Lord sent *"fiery serpents among the people, and they bit the people; and much people of Israel died"* (Num. 21:6). Many have suggested the bite of these serpents were *"fiery"* caused fervent burning upon the victims. Further, it has been argued by many, these serpents were very large (in contrast to the opinions the serpents were but two or three feet in length). Regardless of the size of these serpents, it is clear their bite was often deadly, and for which there was no treatment.

Those bitten were required to look to the serpent made

The Brazen Serpent: A Type of Christ

by Moses to receive healing. Moses made but one serpent, and it was the only source of healing available to the people. In contrast, however, today many look to "*that old serpent the devil*" for refuge and comfort, but in doing so will forever hear the hiss of the serpent throughout eternity, unless they come a knowledge of the truth and obey it (Rev. 12:9 and 20:2).

Those bitten were not to just make visual contact with the serpent Moses placed on the pole to gain their healing, but to gaze upon it with intensity and in full compliance with the Lord's command. Those bitten were to intently gaze upon the serpent with an obedient belief, trust in, and assurance they would be healed. Mere visual contact did not award the needed cure for those bitten. A good study on the phrase "*when he looketh upon it*" provides a clear and distinct picture of the degree of faith required in order to acquire the healing promised by the Lord. God has never awarded man a blessing simply based on mental ascent or visual contact. God has always required man to look to Him with trust and full compliance to His every word.

The Hebrew author wrote:

> *Looking unto Jesus the author and finisher of our faith; who for the joy that was set before him endured the cross, despising the shame, and is set down at the right hand of the throne of God (Heb. 12:2).*

The word *looking* in this passage is akin to the theme and thought of looking upon the serpent. The word means to look intently upon, to look with the eye strongly fixed upon, looking away from all things which distract. So it was the required case regarding those bitten by the fiery serpents. Surely no logically thinking individual would contend that a bitten individual who

All the Types and Shadows of the Old Testament

looked upon the bronze serpent in unbelief would have benefited in any way so far as healing.

Many folks seek the Lord and His favors only when great trials or affliction come upon them and expect God to remedy their problems in haste. The Jews of old were often of the same mindset; for the Scripture states the people "*came to Moses, and said, We have sinned, for we have spoken against the Lord, and against thee; pray unto the Lord, that he take away the serpents from us. And Moses prayed for the people*" (Num. 21:7). It is sad so many seek access to God as a last resort, but such is nonetheless true. Consider the following ways in which this incident paints pictures for the Bible student.

1. The Israelites spoke ill of the Lord and Moses because the lack of water and food (Num. 21:5).

Many saints speak ill of the Lord for lack of things they desire, and fail to realize the kingdom is more than food and drink (Matt. 4:4; 6:25; Luke 12:23,

2. The fiery serpents inflicted the Israelites with burning poison, causing physical death, Num. 21:6; I Cor. 10:9).

Satan, the old serpent the Devil inflicts the church with the poison of sin (John 8:44; Rev. 12:9).

3. The brazen serpent was lifted up on a pole (Num. 21:8).

Christ was lifted up on the cross (John 3:14-15; Acts 2:23).

The Brazen Serpent: A Type of Christ

4. There was but one serpent to which the Israelites could look intently to secure the needed remedy (Num. 21:8).

There is but one savior to whom man must look to acquire salvation (Eph. 1:22-23; 4:5; Acts 4:12; I Cor. 3:11; Heb. 5:8-9).

5. The news of the healing serpent had to be broadcast (Num. 21:8).

The good news of the gospel must be broadcast to all (Mark 16:15-16; Luke 24:47–50; Rom. 10:13–17).

6. None of the Israelites were forced to look upon the serpent (Num. 21:8).

Man is not forced to obey the gospel (II Thes. 1:6–9; Rom. 10:16; Gal. 3:1; 5:7; I Pet. 2:8).

7. The Israelites were not healed by faith only (Num. 21:8-9).

Men today are not save by faith only (John 12:42-43; Jas. 2:14–26).

8. The Israelites were to obey the command to look intently on the brazen serpent to receive healing (Num. 21:8.9).

Men today must obey the Lord to receive healing (John 14:15; 15:14; Heb. 5:9).

9. The Israelites could not be physically healed by prayer (Num. 21:8).

Sinful men today cannot be spiritually saved by prayer (John 9:31).

All the Types and Shadows of the Old Testament

10. That some Israelites died in disobedience did not negate the power of healing God provided, for those who obeyed *were* healed.

Disobedience to God's law today does not negate the power of the gospel (Rom. 9:6; Gal. 3:17).

The Cities of Refuge: Types of the Church

The cities of refuge are seldom given the recognition they deserve. Not many are aware the six cities of refuge serve as types of the Lord's church. Numerous verses address the cities of refuge, which are provided hereafter.

> And the LORD spake unto Moses, saying, Speak unto the children of Israel, and say unto them, When ye be come over Jordan into the land of Canaan; then ye shall appoint you cities to be cities of refuge for you; that the slayer may flee thither, which killeth any person at unawares. And they shall be unto you cities for refuge from the avenger; that the manslayer die not, until he stand before the congregation in judgment.
>
> And of these cities which ye shall give six cities shall ye have for refuge. Ye shall give three cities on this side Jordan, and three cities shall ye give in the land of Canaan, which shall be cities of refuge. These six cities shall be a refuge, both for the children of Israel, and for the stranger, and for the sojourner among them: that every one that killeth any person unawares may flee thither.
>
> And if he smite him with an instrument of iron, so that he die, he is a murderer: the murderer shall surely be put to death. And if he smite him with throwing a stone, wherewith he may die, and he die, he is a murderer: the murderer shall surely be put to death. Or if he smite him with an hand weapon of wood, wherewith he may die, and he

All the Types and Shadows of the Old Testament

die, he is a murderer: the murderer shall surely be put to death. The revenger of blood himself shall slay the murderer: when he meeteth him, he shall slay him.

But if he thrust him of hatred, or hurl at him by laying of wait, that he die; or in enmity smite him with his hand, that he die: he that smote him shall surely be put to death; for he is a murderer: the revenger of blood shall slay the murderer, when he meeteth him.

But if he thrust him suddenly without enmity, or have cast upon him any thing without laying of wait, or with any stone, wherewith a man may die, seeing him not, and cast it upon him, that he die, and was not his enemy, neither sought his harm: then the congregation shall judge between the slayer and the revenger of blood according to these judgments: and the congregation shall deliver the slayer out of the hand of the revenger of blood, and the congregation shall restore him to the city of his refuge, whither he was fled: and he shall abide in it unto the death of the high priest, which was anointed with the holy oil.

But if the slayer shall at any time come without the border of the city of his refuge, whither he was fled; and the revenger of blood find him without the borders of the city of his refuge, and the revenger of blood kill the slayer; he shall not be guilty of blood: because he should have remained in the city of his refuge until the death of the high priest: but after the death of the high priest the slayer shall return into the land of his possession.

So these things shall be for a statute of judgment unto you throughout your generations in all your dwellings. Whoso killeth any person, the murderer shall be put to death by the mouth of

The Cities of Refuge: Types of the Church

witnesses: but one witness shall not testify against any person to cause him to die. Moreover ye shall take no satisfaction for the life of a murderer, which is guilty of death: but he shall be surely put to death. And ye shall take no satisfaction for him that is fled to the city of his refuge, that he should come again to dwell in the land, until the death of the priest.

So ye shall not pollute the land wherein ye are: for blood it defileth the land: and the land cannot be cleansed of the blood that is shed therein, but by the blood of him that shed it. Defile not therefore the land which ye shall inhabit, wherein I dwell: for I the LORD dwell among the children of Israel (Num. 35:9–34).

Then Moses severed three cities on this side Jordan toward the sunrising; that the slayer might flee thither, which should kill his neighbor unawares, and hated him not in times past; and that fleeing unto one of these cities he might live: Namely, Bezer in the wilderness, in the plain country, of the Reubenites; and Ramoth in Gilead, of the Gadites; and Golan in Bashan, of the Manassites (Deut. 4:41–43).

The Lord also spake unto Joshua, saying, Speak to the children of Israel, saying, Appoint out for you cities of refuge, whereof I spake unto you by the hand of Moses: That the slayer that killeth any person unawares and unwittingly may flee thither: and they shall be your refuge from the avenger of blood. And when he that doth flee unto one of those cities shall stand at the entering of the gate of the city, and shall declare his cause in the ears of the elders of that city, they shall take him into the city unto them, and give him a place, that he may dwell among them. And if the avenger

All the Types and Shadows of the Old Testament

of blood pursue after him, then they shall not deliver the slayer up into his hand; because he smote his neighbour unwittingly, and hated him not beforetime. And he shall dwell in that city, until he stand before the congregation for judgment, and until the death of the high priest that shall be in those days: then shall the slayer return, and come unto his own city, and unto his own house, unto the city from whence he fled.

And they appointed Kedesh in Galilee in mount Naphtali, and Shechem in mount Ephraim, and Kirjatharba, which is Hebron, in the mountain of Judah. And on the other side Jordan by Jericho eastward, they assigned Bezer in the wilderness upon the plain out of the tribe of Reuben, and Ramoth in Gilead out of the tribe of Gad, and Golan in Bashan out of the tribe of Manasseh. These were the cities appointed for all the children of Israel, and for the stranger that sojourneth among them, that whosoever killeth any person at unawares might flee thither, and not die by the hand of the avenger of blood, until he stood before the congregation. (Josh. 20:1–10).

Now king David was old and stricken in years; and they covered him with clothes, but he gat no heat. Wherefore his servants said unto him, Let there be sought for my Lord the king a young virgin: and let her stand before the king, and let her cherish him, and let her lie in thy bosom, that my Lord the king may get heat. So they sought for a fair damsel throughout all the coasts of Israel, and found Abishag a Shunammite, and brought her to the king. And the damsel was very fair, and cherished the king, and ministered to him: but the king knew her not.

Then Adonijah the son of Haggith exalted himself, saying, I will be king: and he prepared him

The Cities of Refuge: Types of the Church

chariots and horsemen, and fifty men to run before him. And his father had not displeased him at any time in saying, Why hast thou done so? and he also was a very goodly man; and his mother bare him after Absalom. And he conferred with Joab the son of Zeruiah, and with Abiathar the priest: and they following Adonijah helped him.

But Zadok the priest, and Benaiah the son of Jehoiada, and Nathan the prophet, and Shimei, and Rei, and the mighty men which belonged to David, were not with Adonijah.

And Adonijah slew sheep and oxen and fat cattle by the stone of Zoheleth, which is by Enrogel, and called all his brethren the king's sons, and all the men of Judah the king's servants. But Nathan the prophet, and Benaiah, and the mighty men, and Solomon his brother, he called not.

Wherefore Nathan spake unto Bathsheba the mother of Solomon, saying, Hast thou not heard that Adonijah the son of Haggith doth reign, and David our Lord knoweth it not? Now therefore come, let me, I pray thee, give thee counsel, that thou mayest save thine own life, and the life of thy son Solomon. Go and get thee in unto king David, and say unto him, Didst not thou, my Lord, O king, swear unto thine handmaid, saying, Assuredly Solomon thy son shall reign after me, and he shall sit upon my throne? Why then doth Adonijah reign? Behold, while thou yet talkest there with the king, I also will come in after thee, and confirm thy words.

And Bathsheba went in unto the king into the chamber: and the king was very old; and Abishag the Shunammite ministered unto the king. And Bathsheba bowed, and did obeisance unto the king. And the king said, What wouldest thou? And

All the Types and Shadows of the Old Testament

she said unto him, My Lord, thou swarest by the Lord thy God unto thine handmaid, saying, Assuredly Solomon thy son shall reign after me, and he shall sit upon my throne. And now, behold, Adonijah reigneth; and now, my Lord the king, thou knowest it not: And he hath slain oxen and fat cattle and sheep in abundance, and hath called all the sons of the king, and Abiathar the priest, and Joab the captain of the host: but Solomon thy servant hath he not called. And thou, my Lord, O king, the eyes of all Israel are upon thee, that thou shouldest tell them who shall sit on the throne of my Lord the king after him. Otherwise it shall come to pass, when my Lord the king shall sleep with his fathers, that I and my son Solomon shall be counted offenders.

And, lo, while she yet talked with the king, Nathan the prophet also came in. And they told the king, saying, Behold Nathan the prophet. And when he was come in before the king, he bowed himself before the king with his face to the ground. And Nathan said, My Lord, O king, hast thou said, Adonijah shall reign after me, and he shall sit upon my throne? For he is gone down this day, and hath slain oxen and fat cattle and sheep in abundance, and hath called all the king's sons, and the captains of the host, and Abiathar the priest; and, behold, they eat and drink before him, and say, God save king Adonijah. But me, even me thy servant, and Zadok the priest, and Benaiah the son of Jehoiada, and thy servant Solomon, hath he not called. Is this thing done by my Lord the king, and thou hast not shewed it unto thy servant, who should sit on the throne of my Lord the king after him?

Then king David answered and said, Call me

The Cities of Refuge: Types of the Church

Bathsheba. And she came into the king's presence, and stood before the king. And the king sware, and said, As the Lord liveth, that hath redeemed my soul out of all distress, Even as I sware unto thee by the Lord God of Israel, saying, Assuredly Solomon thy son shall reign after me, and he shall sit upon my throne in my stead; even so will I certainly do this day.

Then Bathsheba bowed with her face to the earth, and did reverence to the king, and said, Let my Lord king David live for ever.

And king David said, Call me Zadok the priest, and Nathan the prophet, and Benaiah the son of Jehoiada. And they came before the king. The king also said unto them, Take with you the servants of your Lord, and cause Solomon my son to ride upon mine own mule, and bring him down to Gihon: And let Zadok the priest and Nathan the prophet anoint him there king over Israel: and blow ye with the trumpet, and say, God save king Solomon. Then ye shall come up after him, that he may come and sit upon my throne; for he shall be king in my stead: and I have appointed him to be ruler over Israel and over Judah.

And Benaiah the son of Jehoiada answered the king, and said, Amen: the Lord God of my Lord the king say so too. As the Lord hath been with my Lord the king, even so be he with Solomon, and make his throne greater than the throne of my Lord king David.

So Zadok the priest, and Nathan the prophet, and Benaiah the son of Jehoiada, and the Cherethites, and the Pelethites, went down, and caused Solomon to ride upon king David's mule, and brought him to Gihon. And Zadok the priest took an horn of oil out of the tabernacle, and anointed

All the Types and Shadows of the Old Testament

Solomon. And they blew the trumpet; and all the people said, God save king Solomon. And all the people came up after him, and the people piped with pipes, and rejoiced with great joy, so that the earth rent with the sound of them.

And Adonijah and all the guests that were with him heard it as they had made an end of eating. And when Joab heard the sound of the trumpet, he said, Wherefore is this noise of the city being in an uproar?

And while he yet spake, behold, Jonathan the son of Abiathar the priest came: and Adonijah said unto him, Come in; for thou art a valiant man, and bringest good tidings.

And Jonathan answered and said to Adonijah, Verily our Lord king David hath made Solomon king. And the king hath sent with him Zadok the priest, and Nathan the prophet, and Benaiah the son of Jehoiada, and the Cherethites, and the Pelethites, and they have caused him to ride upon the king's mule: And Zadok the priest and Nathan the prophet have anointed him king in Gihon: and they are come up from thence rejoicing, so that the city rang again. This is the noise that ye have heard. And also Solomon sitteth on the throne of the kingdom. And moreover the king's servants came to bless our Lord king David, saying, God make the name of Solomon better than thy name, and make his throne greater than thy throne. And the king bowed himself upon the bed. And also thus said the king, Blessed be the Lord God of Israel, which hath given one to sit on my throne this day, mine eyes even seeing it.

And all the guests that were with Adonijah were afraid, and rose up, and went every man his way. And Adonijah feared because of Solomon, and

The Cities of Refuge: Types of the Church

arose, and went, and caught hold on the horns of the altar. And it was told Solomon, saying, Behold, Adonijah feareth king Solomon: for, lo, he hath caught hold on the horns of the altar, saying, Let king Solomon swear unto me to day that he will not slay his servant with the sword.

And Solomon said, If he will shew himself a worthy man, there shall not an hair of him fall to the earth: but if wickedness shall be found in him, he shall die. So king Solomon sent, and they brought him down from the altar. And he came and bowed himself to king Solomon: and Solomon said unto him, Go to thine house (I Kings 1:1–53).

The Hebrew author alluded to the cities of refuge, saying, "*That by two immutable things, in which it was impossible for God to lie, we might have a strong consolation, who have fled for refuge to lay hold upon the hope set before us*" (Heb. 6:18).

The locations of the six cities of refuge were located strategically. The names of the cities of Cities of Refuge each have unique meaning. The meanings of these cities spell out some of the spiritual blessings of comfort Christians find in the Lord's church (Eph. 1:3).

Kadesh means *holy place* or *righteousness*. The Lord's church is a place of holiness wherein Christians are made holy. Peter wrote: "*Because it is written, Be ye holy; for I am holy*" (I Pet. 1:16).

Shechem means *shoulder* or *a place of strength*. Paul wrote: "*Finally, my brethren, be strong in the Lord, and in the power of his might*" (Eph. 6:10).

Hebron means *fellowship*. John wrote: "*But if we walk in the light, as he is in the light, we have fellowship one with another, and the blood of Jesus Christ his Son*

All the Types and Shadows of the Old Testament

cleanseth us from all sin" (I John 1:7).

Bezer means *stronghold, fortress,* or *a fortified place.* David said: "*The Lord is my rock, and my fortress, and my deliverer; my God, my strength, in whom I will trust; my buckler, and the horn of my salvation, and my high tower*" (Psa. 18:2).

Ramoth means *exalted* or *height.* The Lord said: "*For whosoever exalteth himself shall be abased; and he that humbleth himself shall be exalted*" (Luke 14:11).

Golan means *joy* or *exultation.* "*But rejoice, inasmuch as ye are partakers of Christ's sufferings; that, when his glory shall be revealed, ye may be glad also with exceeding joy*" (I Pet. 4:13).

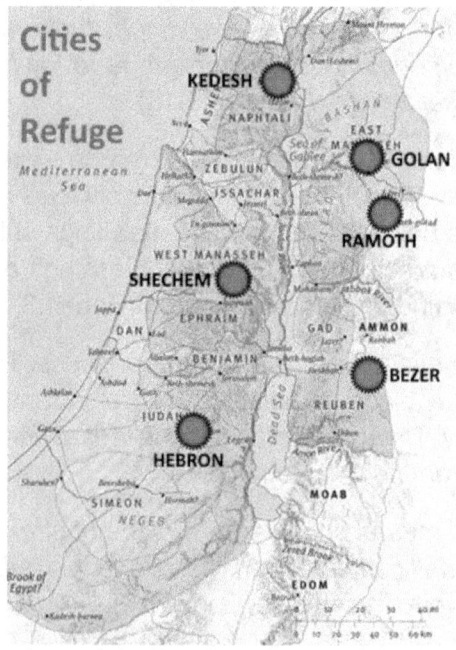

Consider the comparisons and contrasts between the cities of refuge that serve as types and anti-types of the church.

The Cities of Refuge: Types of the Church

1. The cities of refuge were provided as a safe haven for those fleeing the avenger of blood (Josh. 20:9).

Men must flee from their adversary their Devil, who seeks to devour them (I Pet. 5:8).

2. The cities of refuge were for both the children of Israel and the stranger (Num. 35:15).

The salvation Christ provides is for both the penitent Christian and the alien sinner (Matt. 28:19; Eph. 2:14–16; I Cor. 15:1-3).

3. Access to the cities of refuge was well prepared and plain (Deut. 19:3).

The way of salvation has been prepared and made easy to access (Isa. 40:3; Mal. 3:1; Matt. 3:1–3).

4. Once in the city of refuge, those who fled thereunto had to remain until the death of the High Priest (Num. 35:24–28).

Those who acquire salvation must remain faithful in the Lord's church until they die (John 15:1–6; Gal. 5:4; Heb. 7:23-28; Rev. 2:10).

5. The cities of refuge provided salvation from physical death (Num. 35:11–34).

Spiritual death is averted in the Lord's church when one remains faithful (John 11:25; 14:6).

All the Types and Shadows of the Old Testament

The Two Goats: A Type of Christ

Few are aware of the two goats recorded in Leviticus 16 which serve as a type of Christ.

> *And he shall take the two goats, and present them before the Lord at the door of the tabernacle of the congregation. And Aaron shall cast lots upon the two goats; one lot for the Lord, and the other lot for the scapegoat. And Aaron shall bring the goat upon which the Lord's lot fell, and offer him for a sin offering. But the goat, on which the lot fell to be the scapegoat, shall be presented*

All the Types and Shadows of the Old Testament

alive before the Lord, to make an atonement with him, and to let him go for a scapegoat into the wilderness.

And Aaron shall bring the bullock of the sin offering, which is for himself, and shall make an atonement for himself, and for his house, and shall kill the bullock of the sin offering which is for himself: And he shall take a censer full of burning coals of fire from off the altar before the Lord, and his hands full of sweet incense beaten small, and bring it within the vail: And he shall put the incense upon the fire before the Lord, that the cloud of the incense may cover the mercy seat that is upon the testimony, that he die not.

And he shall take of the blood of the bullock, and sprinkle it with his finger upon the mercy seat eastward; and before the mercy seat shall he sprinkle of the blood with his finger seven times.

Then shall he kill the goat of the sin offering, that is for the people, and bring his blood within the vail, and do with that blood as he did with the blood of the bullock, and sprinkle it upon the mercy seat, and before the mercy seat:

And he shall make an atonement for the holy place, because of the uncleanness of the children of Israel, and because of their transgressions in all their sins: and so shall he do for the tabernacle of the congregation, that remaineth among them in the midst of their uncleanness.

And there shall be no man in the tabernacle of the congregation when he goeth in to make an atonement in the holy place, until he come out, and have made an atonement for himself, and for his household, and for all the congregation of Israel. And he shall go out unto the altar that is before the Lord, and make an atonement for it; and

The Two Goats: Types of Christ

shall take of the blood of the bullock, and of the blood of the goat, and put it upon the horns of the altar round about. And he shall sprinkle of the blood upon it with his finger seven times, and cleanse it, and hallow it from the uncleanness of the children of Israel.

And when he hath made an end of reconciling the holy place, and the tabernacle of the congregation, and the altar, he shall bring the live goat: And Aaron shall lay both his hands upon the head of the live goat, and confess over him all the iniquities of the children of Israel, and all their transgressions in all their sins, putting them upon the head of the goat, and shall send him away by the hand of a fit man into the wilderness: And the goat shall bear upon him all their iniquities unto a land not inhabited: and he shall let go the goat in the wilderness (Lev. 16:7–22).

It is needful to consider the two goats together to properly understand how they serve as Christ in type. One goat was slain, which represents Christ having been slain on our behalf. The High Priest was to take the blood of the slain goat and sprinkle it upon the Mercy Seat within the Most Holy Place. Seven times the blood was sprinkled—seven represents purity and perfection. The blood of Christ was the cleansing agent designated by the Lord to serve as the complete atoning offering on behalf of man.

The other goat had the sins of the people confessed upon it and was to be removed from the camp. Both hands of the High Priest were laid upon that goat which was a display of trust in God's forgiveness (Lev. 16:20–22). This was done once every year: Consider:

All the Types and Shadows of the Old Testament

> And this shall be an everlasting statute unto you, to make an atonement for the children of Israel for all their sins once a year. And he did as the Lord commanded Moses (Exo. 16:34).
>
> For the law having a shadow of good things to come, and not the very image of the things, can never with those sacrifices which they offered year by year continually make the comers thereunto perfect. For then would they not have ceased to be offered? because that the worshippers once purged should have had no more conscience of sins. But in those sacrifices there is a remembrance again made of sins every year. For it is not possible that the blood of bulls and of goats should take away sins (Heb. 10:1–4).

1. The goat which was to be slain was chosen by the casting of lots which was determined by the Lord (Lev. 16:7–10; Prov. 16:33).

God chose Christ to be the sacrifice for man (Rom. 5:8–11).

2. The blood of the sacrificed goat was sprinkled on the Mercy Seat for the atonement of Israel (Lev. 16:15-16).

Christ made atonement for man with His blood (Rom. 5:8–11; I Pet. 1:18-19).

3. Only the High Priest was authorized to enter the Most Holy Place when the blood of the slain goat was sprinkled on the Mercy Seat, thus making atonement for the Israelites (Lev. 16:17).

Christ made atonement for our sins by shedding His blood and is now in heaven at the right hand of the Father (Rom. 8:34; Acts 2:33; Heb. 12:2).

The Two Goats: Types of Christ

4. The High Priest sprinkled the sacrificial blood seven times, signifying the completeness of the cleansing for the Israelites (Lev. 16:19).

Christ made a complete atonement for our sins (Heb. 10:9-10).

5. Over the head of the living goat the sins of the people were confessed (Lev. 16:20–22).

Upon the head of Christ was placed a crown of thorns which He bore to make restitution for our sins (Isa. 53:4; 5; John 19:2, 5).

6. Both hands of the High Priest upon the head of the scapegoat represented trust in the Lord's willingness to pardon the people (Lev. 16:20–22).

Christians are to have unwavering faith that through the sacrifice of Christ our sins are forgiven (Rom. 6:16–18).

7. The mandate for the two goats was that it be done once every year (Lev. 16:31; Heb. 10:1–4).

Christ was sacrificed once for all time (Rom. 8:3; Heb. 10:10; I Pet. 3:18).

8. The two goats serves as substitutes for Israel (Lev. 16:15).

Christ suffered for us, the just for the unjust (Heb. 9:28; I Pet. 3:18).

9. The scapegoat was cast out of the camp (Lev. 16:10).

Christ was crucified outside the city (Matt. 27:32-33).

10. The scapegoat led out of the camp (Lev. 16:21).

Christ was led out of the city (Mark 15:22; John 19:17).

All the Types and Shadows of the Old Testament

Leprosy:
A Type of Sin

And the Lord spake unto Moses, saying, This shall be the law of the leper in the day of his cleansing: He shall be brought unto the priest: And the priest shall go forth out of the camp; and the priest shall look, and, behold, if the plague of leprosy be healed in the leper, then shall the priest command to take for him that is to be cleansed two birds alive and clean, and cedar wood, and scarlet, and hyssop: And the priest shall command that one of the birds be killed in an earthen vessel over running water: As for the living bird, he shall take it, and the cedar wood, and the scarlet, and the hyssop, and shall dip them and the living bird in the blood of the bird that was killed over the running water: And he shall sprinkle upon him that is to be cleansed from the leprosy seven times, and shall pronounce him clean, and shall let the living bird loose into the open field.

And he that is to be cleansed shall wash his clothes, and shave off all his hair, and wash himself in water, that he may be clean: and after that he shall come into the camp, and shall tarry abroad out of his tent seven days. But it shall be on the seventh day, that he shall shave all his hair off his head and his beard and his eyebrows, even all his hair he shall shave off: and he shall wash his clothes, also he shall wash his flesh in water, and he shall be clean.

And on the eighth day he shall take two he lambs without blemish, and one ewe lamb of the

All the Types and Shadows of the Old Testament

first year without blemish, and three tenth deals of fine flour for a meat offering, mingled with oil, and one log of oil.

And the priest that maketh him clean shall present the man that is to be made clean, and those things, before the Lord, at the door of the tabernacle of the congregation: And the priest shall take one he lamb, and offer him for a trespass offering, and the log of oil, and wave them for a wave offering before the Lord: And he shall slay the lamb in the place where he shall kill the sin offering and the burnt offering, in the holy place: for as the sin offering is the priest's, so is the trespass offering: it is most holy:

And the priest shall take some of the blood of the trespass offering, and the priest shall put it upon the tip of the right ear of him that is to be cleansed, and upon the thumb of his right hand, and upon the great toe of his right foot: And the priest shall take some of the log of oil, and pour it into the palm of his own left hand: And the priest shall dip his right finger in the oil that is in his left hand, and shall sprinkle of the oil with his finger seven times before the Lord: And of the rest of the oil that is in his hand shall the priest put upon the tip of the right ear of him that is to be cleansed, and upon the thumb of his right hand, and upon the great toe of his right foot, upon the blood of the trespass offering: And the remnant of the oil that is in the priest's hand he shall pour upon the head of him that is to be cleansed: and the priest shall make an atonement for him before the Lord.

And the priest shall offer the sin offering, and make an atonement for him that is to be cleansed from his uncleanness; and afterward he shall kill the burnt offering: And the priest shall offer the burnt offering and the meat offering upon the altar:

Leprosy: A Type of Sin

and the priest shall make an atonement for him, and he shall be clean.

And if he be poor, and cannot get so much; then he shall take one lamb for a trespass offering to be waved, to make an atonement for him, and one tenth deal of fine flour mingled with oil for a meat offering, and a log of oil; and two turtledoves, or two young pigeons, such as he is able to get; and the one shall be a sin offering, and the other a burnt offering. And he shall bring them on the eighth day for his cleansing unto the priest, unto the door of the tabernacle of the congregation, before the Lord.

And the priest shall take the lamb of the trespass offering, and the log of oil, and the priest shall wave them for a wave offering before the Lord: And he shall kill the lamb of the trespass offering, and the priest shall take some of the blood of the trespass offering, and put it upon the tip of the right ear of him that is to be cleansed, and upon the thumb of his right hand, and upon the great toe of his right foot: And the priest shall pour of the oil into the palm of his own left hand: And the priest shall sprinkle with his right finger some of the oil that is in his left hand seven times before the Lord: And the priest shall put of the oil that is in his hand upon the tip of the right ear of him that is to be cleansed, and upon the thumb of his right hand, and upon the great toe of his right foot, upon the place of the blood of the trespass offering: And the rest of the oil that is in the priest's hand he shall put upon the head of him that is to be cleansed, to make an atonement for him before the Lord.

And he shall offer the one of the turtledoves, or of the young pigeons, such as he can get; Even such as he is able to get, the one for a sin offering,

All the Types and Shadows of the Old Testament

and the other for a burnt offering, with the meat offering: and the priest shall make an atonement for him that is to be cleansed before the Lord. This is the law of him in whom is the plague of leprosy, whose hand is not able to get that which pertaineth to his cleansing.

And the Lord spake unto Moses and unto Aaron, saying, When ye be come into the land of Canaan, which I give to you for a possession, and I put the plague of leprosy in a house of the land of your possession; and he that owneth the house shall come and tell the priest, saying, It seemeth to me there is as it were a plague in the house: Then the priest shall command that they empty the house, before the priest go into it to see the plague, that all that is in the house be not made unclean: and afterward the priest shall go in to see the house.

And he shall look on the plague, and, behold, if the plague be in the walls of the house with hollow strakes, greenish or reddish, which in sight are lower than the wall; Then the priest shall go out of the house to the door of the house, and shut up the house seven days: And the priest shall come again the seventh day, and shall look: and, behold, if the plague be spread in the walls of the house; Then the priest shall command that they take away the stones in which the plague is, and they shall cast them into an unclean place without the city: And he shall cause the house to be scraped within round about, and they shall pour out the dust that they scrape off without the city into an unclean place: And they shall take other stones, and put them in the place of those stones; and he shall take other morter, and shall plaister the house.

Leprosy: A Type of Sin

And if the plague come again, and break out in the house, after that he hath taken away the stones, and after he hath scraped the house, and after it is plaistered; then the priest shall come and look, and, behold, if the plague be spread in the house, it is a fretting leprosy in the house: it is unclean. And he shall break down the house, the stones of it, and the timber thereof, and all the morter of the house; and he shall carry them forth out of the city into an unclean place. Moreover he that goeth into the house all the while that it is shut up shall be unclean until the even. And he that lieth in the house shall wash his clothes; and he that eateth in the house shall wash his clothes.

And if the priest shall come in, and look upon it, and, behold, the plague hath not spread in the house, after the house was plaistered: then the priest shall pronounce the house clean, because the plague is healed. And he shall take to cleanse the house two birds, and cedar wood, and scarlet, and hyssop: And he shall kill the one of the birds in an earthen vessel over running water: And he shall take the cedar wood, and the hyssop, and the scarlet, and the living bird, and dip them in the blood of the slain bird, and in the running water, and sprinkle the house seven times: And he shall cleanse the house with the blood of the bird, and with the running water, and with the living bird, and with the cedar wood, and with the hyssop, and with the scarlet: But he shall let go the living bird out of the city into the open fields, and make an atonement for the house: and it shall be clean.

This is the law for all manner of plague of leprosy, and scall, And for the leprosy of a garment, and of a house, And for a rising, and for a scab, and for a bright spot: to teach when it is unclean,

All the Types and Shadows of the Old Testament

and when it is clean: this is the law of leprosy (Lev. 14:1–57).

Leprosy is a subject well known to most Bible students, but few understand how it serves in type. There are two chapters in the Leviticus which record laws concerning leprosy; chapters 13 and 14. Chapter 13 deals with laws about leprosy itself, and chapter 14 addresses the laws regarding the leper (vss. 1–32). Laws pertaining the cleansing of the homes of lepers are found in the remainder of the chapter (vss. 33–57).

Leprosy was a disease which had no cure. On a few rare occasions one was fortunate to have his leprosy cured through the body's ability to ward off the disease. Leprosy is a disease eats away the flesh. Consider the images below.

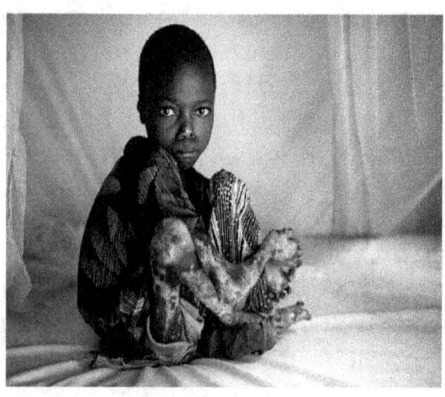
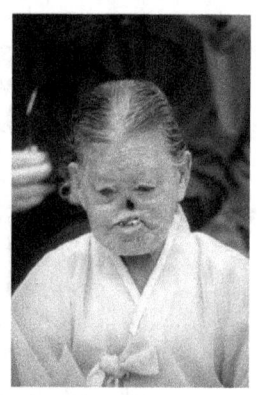

Leprosy was a disease which made one unclean and unfit to be a part of the society of healthy individuals; it had no human cure. Lepers were required to cover their mouths and cry "Unclean" whenever a non-leprous person came near (Lev. 13:34-35. Lepers were always in agonizing pain. Lepers often lost fingers, toes, arms, feet nose and ears, such members falling off at the joints. Uncured leprosy resulted in an agonizing death.

Leprosy: A Type of Sin

For those who were fortunate enough to be cured of leprosy through the body's ability to fight off the disease, they were to go and show themselves to the priests, who would make the declaration of cleanness from the disease, Lev. 14:1–22).

1. Leprosy was treated both as a disease and as uncleanness (Lev. 13).
Sin is the disease of the soul making the soul unclean (II Cor. 7:1).

2. Leprosy corrupts the purity of the victim's blood and is very contagious.
Sin is that which defiles a man and stains his hands in the blood of sin (Isa. 1:15; 59:3).

3. Leprosy had no human cure (Lev. 13-14).
Sin has no human cure, but only cured by the blood of Christ (I Cor. 6:11; Heb. 9:14; I Pet. 1:18-19).

4. Leprosy was a contagious disease (Lev. 13-14).
Sin is a disease of the soul and corrupts others (I Cor. 5:6; 15:33).

5. Leprosy is a disease which spreads (Lev. 13-14).
Sin is a disease which spreads (II Tim. 2:17; 3:13).

6. Leprosy is extremely painful (Lev. 13-14; Luke 17:11–19).
Sin is a hard master (Pro. 13:15; Gal. 6:7).

7. Lepers were cast out of the company of God's people (Lev. 13:45-46).
Sinning members of the Lord's church are cast out from among God's people (I Cor. 5:1–11; II Thes. 3:6).

All the Types and Shadows of the Old Testament

8. Uncured leprosy results in a miserable death (Lev. 13-14).

Uncured sin results in a miserable spiritual death (Jas. 1:13–15).

9. The Lord chose to save some from leprosy (II Kings 5:1–14; Matt. 8:1–4; Luke 17:11–19).

The Lord saves men from the leprosy of sin (John 5:40; 6:47; Matt. 7:21; Heb. 5:8-9).

10. Lepers had to offer a sacrifice for their cleansing (Lev. 14:1–22; Mark 1:44).

Those cleansed of the leprosy of sin are to offer themselves in the service of the Lord (Rom. 6:17; 12:2; I Pet. 2:5).

11. The priest was the only one who was authorized to pronounce one cleansed of leprosy (Lev. 14:1–22).

Only Christ has the power to declare spiritual lepers cleansed from sin (Heb. 4:15-16; 10:19–22).

The Sabbatical Year and the Year of Jubilee: Types of the Gospel Age

The Sabbatical years of rest for the land of Israel and the year of Jubilee are subjects filled with immense intensity. However, in order to best ascertain how the Sabbatical years and the year of Jubilee serve as a type of the Gospel era, it is essential have an overall history and knowledge of both.

> *And the Lord spake unto Moses in mount Sinai, saying, Speak unto the children of Israel, and say unto them, When ye come into the land which I give you, then shall the land keep a sabbath unto the Lord. Six years thou shalt sow thy field, and six years thou shalt prune thy vineyard, and gather in the fruit thereof; But in the seventh year shall be a sabbath of rest unto the land, a sabbath for the Lord: thou shalt neither sow thy field, nor prune thy vineyard. That which groweth of its own accord of thy harvest thou shalt not reap, neither gather the grapes of thy vine undressed: for it is a year of rest unto the land.*
>
> *And the sabbath of the land shall be meat for you; for thee, and for thy servant, and for thy maid, and for thy hired servant, and for thy stranger that sojourneth with thee, and for thy cattle, and for the beast that are in thy land, shall all the increase thereof be meat.*
>
> *And thou shalt number seven sabbaths of years unto thee, seven times seven years; and*

All the Types and Shadows of the Old Testament

the space of the seven sabbaths of years shall be unto thee forty and nine years. Then shalt thou cause the trumpet of the jubilee to sound on the tenth day of the seventh month, in the day of atonement shall ye make the trumpet sound throughout all your land. And ye shall hallow the fiftieth year, and proclaim liberty throughout all the land unto all the inhabitants thereof: it shall be a jubilee unto you; and ye shall return every man unto his possession, and ye shall return every man unto his family.

A jubilee shall that fiftieth year be unto you: ye shall not sow, neither reap that which groweth of itself in it, nor gather the grapes in it of thy vine undressed. For it is the jubilee; it shall be holy unto you: ye shall eat the increase thereof out of the field. In the year of this jubilee ye shall return every man unto his possession.

And if thou sell ought unto thy neighbour, or buyest ought of thy neighbour's hand, ye shall not oppress one another: According to the number of years after the jubilee thou shalt buy of thy neighbour, and according unto the number of years of the fruits he shall sell unto thee: According to the multitude of years thou shalt increase the price thereof, and according to the fewness of years thou shalt diminish the price of it: for according to the number of the years of the fruits doth he sell unto thee. Ye shall not therefore oppress one another; but thou shalt fear thy God: for I am the Lord your God.

Wherefore ye shall do my statutes, and keep my judgments, and do them; and ye shall dwell in the land in safety. And the land shall yield her fruit, and ye shall eat your fill, and dwell therein in safety. And if ye shall say, What shall we eat the seventh year? behold, we shall not sow, nor

The Sabbatical Year and Year of Jubilee

> *gather in our increase: Then I will command my blessing upon you in the sixth year, and it shall bring forth fruit for three years. And ye shall sow the eighth year, and eat yet of old fruit until the ninth year; until her fruits come in ye shall eat of the old store (Lev. 25:8–22).*

The Jews went into captivity because of their apostasy, which included idolatry and wickedness. There is no Biblical record of the Jews *ever* having kept the Sabbatical years of giving the land her rest, nor is there any record of the Jews having kept the year of Jubilee.

The Lord issued numerous warnings to the Jews if they refused to obey Him. Here our focus is on their failing to keep the Sabbatical years and the year of Jubilee. Consider the following passages (with emphasis) in which the matter of the Jews being subjected to seventy years in Babylonian captivity are recorded.

> *And if ye will not for all this hearken unto me, but walk contrary unto me; Then I will walk contrary unto you also in fury; and I, even I, will chastise you seven times for your sins. And ye shall eat the flesh of your sons, and the flesh of your daughters shall ye eat. And I will destroy your high places, and cut down your images, and cast your carcases upon the carcases of your idols, and my soul shall abhor you. And I will make your cities waste, and bring your sanctuaries unto desolation, and I will not smell the savour of your sweet odours.*
>
> *And I will bring the land into desolation: and your enemies which dwell therein shall be astonished at it. <u>And I will scatter you among the heathen</u>, and will draw out a sword after you: and your land shall be desolate, and your cities waste. <u>Then shall the land enjoy her sabbaths, as long</u>*

All the Types and Shadows of the Old Testament

<u>as it lieth desolate,</u> and ye be in your enemies' land; <u>even then shall the land rest, and enjoy her sabbaths. As long as it lieth desolate it shall rest; because it did not rest in your sabbaths, when ye dwelt upon it.</u>

And upon them that are left alive of you I will send a faintness into their hearts in the lands of their enemies; and the sound of a shaken leaf shall chase them; and they shall flee, as fleeing from a sword; and they shall fall when none pursueth. And they shall fall one upon another, as it were before a sword, when none pursueth: and ye shall have no power to stand before your enemies. And ye shall perish among the heathen, and the land of your enemies shall eat you up.

And they that are left of you shall pine away in their iniquity in your enemies' lands; and also in the iniquities of their fathers shall they pine away with them. If they shall confess their iniquity, and the iniquity of their fathers, with their trespass which they trespassed against me, and that also they have walked contrary unto me; and that I also have walked contrary unto them, and have brought them into the land of their enemies; if then their uncircumcised hearts be humbled, and they then accept of the punishment of their iniquity, then will I remember my covenant with Jacob, and also my covenant with Isaac, and also my covenant with Abraham will I remember; and I will remember the land.

<u>The land also shall be left of them, and shall enjoy her sabbaths</u>, while she lieth desolate without them: and they shall accept of the punishment of their iniquity: because, even because they despised my judgments, and because their soul abhorred my statutes. And yet for all that, when they be in the land of their enemies, I will not cast them

The Sabbatical Year and Year of Jubilee

away, neither will I abhor them, to destroy them utterly, and to break my covenant with them: for I am the Lord their God. But I will for their sakes remember the covenant of their ancestors, whom I brought forth out of the land of Egypt in the sight of the heathen, that I might be their God: I am the Lord. These are the statutes and judgments and laws, which the Lord made between him and the children of Israel in mount Sinai by the hand of Moses (Lev. 26:26–46).

To fulfil the word of the Lord by the mouth of Jeremiah, <u>until the land had enjoyed her sabbaths: for as long as she lay desolate she kept sabbath, to fulfil threescore and ten years</u> (II Chro. 36:21).

In the first year of Darius the son of Ahasuerus, of the seed of the Medes, which was made king over the realm of the Chaldeans. In the first year of his reign <u>I Daniel understood by books the number of the years, whereof the word of the Lord came to Jeremiah the prophet, that he would accomplish seventy years in the desolations of Jerusalem</u> (Dan. 9:1-2)

And this whole land shall be a desolation, and an astonishment; and these nations shall serve the king of Babylon seventy years (Jer. 25:11).

For thus saith the Lord, That after seventy years be accomplished at Babylon I will visit you, and perform my good word toward you, in causing you to return to this place (Jer. 29:10).

Then the angel of the Lord answered and said, <u>O Lord of hosts, how long wilt thou not have mercy on Jerusalem</u> and on the cities of Judah, against which thou hast had indignation these <u>threescore and ten years</u>? (Zec. 1:12).

All the Types and Shadows of the Old Testament

> *Seventy weeks [Years] are determined upon thy people and upon thy holy city, to finish the transgression, and to make an end of sins, and to make reconciliation for iniquity, and to bring in everlasting righteousness, and to seal up the vision and prophecy, and to anoint the most Holy. Know therefore and understand, that from the going forth of the commandment to restore and to build Jerusalem unto the Messiah the Prince shall be seven weeks, and threescore and two weeks: the street shall be built again, and the wall, even in troublous times. And after threescore and two weeks shall Messiah be cut off, but not for himself: and the people of the prince that shall come shall destroy the city and the sanctuary; and the end thereof shall be with a flood, and unto the end of the war desolations are determined. And he shall confirm the covenant with many for one week: and in the midst of the week he shall cause the sacrifice and the oblation to cease, and for the overspreading of abominations he shall make it desolate, even until the consummation, and that determined shall be poured upon the desolate (Dan. 9:24–27).*

While much study is required to ascertain all that encompasses the matter of these passages, we must abridge them here. The Jews were to honor the Sabbath years of the land and keep the year of Jubilee, but we find no record such was ever done, thus the Lord caused the Jews to suffer captivity for a seventy year period. When one calculates time according to the Leviticus passage (chapter 25) cited earlier, it is clear the seventy year period harmonizes perfectly with the seventy years of captivity in Babylon.

Observe the following and how the Sabbatical years and the year of Jubilee serve as a type of the Gospel

The Sabbatical Year and Year of Jubilee

dispensation.

1. All inhabitants of the land of the Jewish nation, whether Jew or foreigners, were to comply with the Sabbatical years and the year of Jubilee (Lev. 25).

All the inhabitants of the earth are to comply with the mandates of the gospel of Christ (Matt. 28:18–20; II Thes. 1:8).

2. The year of Jubilee was a period of mercy extended to the poor and slaves. Slaves were given freedom and the land was restored (Lev. 25).

The gospel era is a period in which God's love for man is awarded to men held captive in sin. Those obedient to the will of the Lord can have their sins remitted and be released from the captivity thereof (Rom. 6:16–18; II Cor. 6:2; Gal. 3:26–29).

3. The year of Jubilee was a time determined and fixed by the Lord (Lev. 25:10).

The gospel dispensation is a time determined by the Lord wherein men may acquire salvation during the reign of Christ.

4. The year of Jubilee was introduced and ushered in on the day atonement, the most sacred day on the Jewish calendar (Lev. 25:9).

The gospel dispensation was introduced when the atoning blood of Christ was shed for the remission of sins (Luke 24:46-47; I Cor. 15:1–4; Rom. 5:11).

5. The year of Jubilee was announced with a joyful sound of the trumpets (Lev. 25:9).

The birth of Christ was announced by the song of angels (Luke 2:8–13).

All the Types and Shadows of the Old Testament

6. The year of Jubilee represented a time of abundance and safety (Lev. 25:18).

The gospel provides abundance and safety (John 10:10; Matt. 11:28–30).

7. The year of Jubilee was a proclamation of liberty from slavery (Lev. 25:39–41).

The gospel of Christ sets obedient men free from the burden of sin (Rom. 6:17-18; Luke 4:18-19).

8. The year of jubilee provided a remission of debts (Lev. 25:39-42).

The gospel of Christ remits the sin of those who obey (Luke 24:46-47; Acts 2:28; 13:38; Rom. 5:8-9).

9. The year of jubilee was a time when all debts were forfeited (Lev. 25).

The blood of Christ in the Christian era provides a forfeiture of spiritual debts (I Cor. 6:11; Heb. 9:14; Rev. 1:5).

10. The year of jubilee was a time of festivity and rest for the land and the people (Lev. 25:11-12).

The gospel era provides rest for those who obey (Matt. 11:28–30).

11. The year of jubilee was given by Moses providing God's grace and physical blessings upon the people (Lev. 25).

The gospel era was given by Christ and provides spiritual blessings and grace upon the obedient (John 1:17; Eph. 1:3).

Joshua: A Type of Christ

Few have considered the man Joshua as a type of Christ, but it is clear Joshua was indeed such. As has been said by numerous men of the book, one should look for Jesus in every passage, He is clearly there.

> Now Joshua son of Nun was filled with the spirit of wisdom because Moses had laid his hands on him. So the Israelites listened to him and did what the Lord had commanded Moses (Deuteronomy 34:9).

Just as Joshua "*was filled with the spirit of wisdom,*" so was Christ. Consider the following: Matt. 13:54; Mark 6:2; Luke 2:40, 52.

All Scripture is given by inspiration of God. Those who were chosen by God were inspired by the Holy Spirit when they were to serve as a type of Christ. Though Joshua is not expressly identified in the New Testament as a type of the Messiah, he is a very eminent type of Christ.

1. Joshua was filled with the spirit of wisdom (Deut. 34:9).

Christ was filled with the Holy Spirit (Matt. 3:16; Isa. 61:1; John 3:34).

All the Types and Shadows of the Old Testament

2. Joshua received a Divine Appointment (Josh. 1:1–5; Num. 27:16–20).

Christ was Divinely appointed (Isa. 42:1; Matt. 10:40; Mark 9:37; Luke 9:48; 10:16; John 4:34; 5:24; 6:38, 40; 7:33; 9:4; 12:44-45; 13:20; 15:21; 16:5; Heb. 1:1–2; 10:9).

3. Joshua's name means savior.
Jesus means savior, Matthew 1:21.

4. Joshua delivered the Jews to the promised land (Josh. 3:1–17).
Jesus will deliver obedient men to the land of promise and rest (Heb. 3:7–4:1).

5. The salvation Joshua provided was physical (Josh. 4:2–24).
The salvation Christ provides is eternal (I Thes. 4:13–18).

6. The salvation of Joshua was but for a few (Josh. 5:6; Deut. 4:2

The salvation of Christ is for all the world, a great multitude which no man can number, Matt. 28:18-20; Rev. 7:9).

7. Joshua was the Successor of Moses (Exo. 24:13
Jesus was Successor to Moses, Matt. 5:17

8. The law was given through Moses, John 1:17).
Grace and truth came through Jesus Christ (John 1:17).

Rahab:
A Type of the Redeemed Church

And Joshua the son of Nun sent out of Shittim two men to spy secretly, saying, Go view the land, even Jericho.

And they went, and came into an harlot's house, named Rahab, and lodged there. And it was told the king of Jericho, saying, Behold, there came men in hither to night of the children of Israel to search out the country. And the king of Jericho sent unto Rahab, saying, Bring forth the men that are come to thee, which are entered into thine house: for they be come to search out all the country.

And the woman took the two men, and hid them, and said thus, There came men unto me, but I wist not whence they were: And it came to pass about the time of shutting of the gate, when it was dark, that the men went out: whither the men went I wot not: pursue after them quickly; for ye shall overtake them. But she had brought them up to the roof of the house, and hid them with the stalks of flax, which she had laid in order upon the roof.

And the men pursued after them the way to Jordan unto the fords: and as soon as they which pursued after them were gone out, they shut the gate.

And before they were laid down, she came up unto them upon the roof; And she said unto the

All the Types and Shadows of the Old Testament

men, I know that the Lord hath given you the land, and that your terror is fallen upon us, and that all the inhabitants of the land faint because of you. For we have heard how the Lord dried up the water of the Red Sea for you, when ye came out of Egypt; and what ye did unto the two kings of the Amorites, that were on the other side Jordan, Sihon and Og, whom ye utterly destroyed. And as soon as we had heard these things, our hearts did melt, neither did there remain any more courage in any man, because of you: for the Lord your God, he is God in heaven above, and in earth beneath. Now therefore, I pray you, swear unto me by the Lord, since I have shewed you kindness, that ye will also shew kindness unto my father's house, and give me a true token: And that ye will save alive my father, and my mother, and my brethren, and my sisters, and all that they have, and deliver our lives from death.

And the men answered her, Our life for yours, if ye utter not this our business. And it shall be, when the LORD hath given us the land, that we will deal kindly and truly with thee.

Then she let them down by a cord through the window: for her house was upon the town wall, and she dwelt upon the wall. And she said unto them, Get you to the mountain, lest the pursuers meet you; and hide yourselves there three days, until the pursuers be returned: and afterward may ye go your way.

And the men said unto her, We will be blameless of this thine oath which thou hast made us swear. Behold, when we come into the land, thou shalt bind this line of scarlet thread in the window which thou didst let us down by: and thou shalt bring thy father, and thy mother, and thy brethren, and all thy father's household, home unto thee.

Rahab: A Type of the Redeemed Church

And it shall be, that whosoever shall go out of the doors of thy house into the street, his blood shall be upon his head, and we will be guiltless: and whosoever shall be with thee in the house, his blood shall be on our head, if any hand be upon him. And if thou utter this our business, then we will be quit of thine oath which thou hast made us to swear.

And she said, According unto your words, so be it. And she sent them away, and they departed: and she bound the scarlet line in the window.

And they went, and came unto the mountain, and abode there three days, until the pursuers were returned: and the pursuers sought them throughout all the way, but found them not. So the two men returned, and descended from the mountain, and passed over, and came to Joshua the son of Nun, and told him all things that befell them: And they said unto Joshua, Truly the Lord hath delivered into our hands all the land; for even all the inhabitants of the country do faint because of us (Josh. 2:1–24).

And the city shall be accursed, even it, and all that are therein, to the Lord: only Rahab the harlot shall live, she and all that are with her in the house, because she hid the messengers that we sent. And ye, in any wise keep yourselves from the accursed thing, lest ye make yourselves accursed, when ye take of the accursed thing, and make the camp of Israel a curse, and trouble it. But all the silver, and gold, and vessels of brass and iron, are consecrated unto the Lord: they shall come into the treasury of the Lord.

So the people shouted when the priests blew with the trumpets: and it came to pass, when the people heard the sound of the trumpet, and the

All the Types and Shadows of the Old Testament

people shouted with a great shout, that the wall fell down flat, so that the people went up into the city, every man straight before him, and they took the city. And they utterly destroyed all that was in the city, both man and woman, young and old, and ox, and sheep, and ass, with the edge of the sword.

But Joshua had said unto the two men that had spied out the country, Go into the harlot's house, and bring out thence the woman, and all that she hath, as ye sware unto her.

And the young men that were spies went in, and brought out Rahab, and her father, and her mother, and her brethren, and all that she had; and they brought out all her kindred, and left them without the camp of Israel. And they burnt the city with fire, and all that was therein: only the silver, and the gold, and the vessels of brass and of iron, they put into the treasury of the house of the Lord.

And Joshua saved Rahab the harlot alive, and her father's household, and all that she had; and she dwelleth in Israel even unto this day; because she hid the messengers, which Joshua sent to spy out Jericho (Josh. 6:17-25).

And Salmon begat Booz of Rachab; and Booz begat Obed of Ruth; and Obed begat Jesse (Matt. 1:5).

By faith the harlot Rahab perished not with them that believed not, when she had received the spies with peace (Heb. 11:31).

Likewise also was not Rahab the harlot justified by works, when she had received the messengers, and had sent them out another way (Jas. 2:25)?

Rahab: A Type of the Redeemed Church

That Rahab is a Bible character to whom little attention is awarded when studying types of the Old Testament is indeed a strong understatement. However, Rahab is given Divine recognition in inspired script in no less than three passages. The apostle Paul declared: *"For whatsoever things were written aforetime were written for our learning, that we through patience and comfort of the scriptures might have hope"* (Rom. 15:4). Further, Paul wrote: *"Now all these things happened unto them for ensamples: and they are written for our admonition, upon whom the ends of the world are come"* (I Cor. 1:11).

We have before us a clear portrait of the bride of Christ in Rahab. Many may take issue with Rahab serving as a type of the church because of the sinful life in which she was involved, being a woman of ill repute. However, each member of the Lord's church (the body of Christ, His bride), was a person of sin before becoming a member thereof. Just as Rahab was awarded salvation from the destruction of Jericho for her obedience, so those obedient to the gospel are granted salvation from the destruction of their souls.

There are numerous passages in New Testament which tell us all men have been poisoned and stained by sin, but may obtain God's redemptive pardon. Consider the following passages which should remind every student of God's word, that all faithful obedient saints were at one time woefully lost in sin, but have been awarded God's gracious forgiveness based upon one's obedience to the gospel.

> *But God commendeth his love toward us, in that, while we were yet sinners, Christ died for us (Rom. 5:9).*

All the Types and Shadows of the Old Testament

> *For God hath concluded them all in unbelief, that he might have mercy upon all (Rom. 11:32).*
>
> *Know ye not that the unrighteous shall not inherit the kingdom of God? Be not deceived: neither fornicators, nor idolaters, nor adulterers, nor effeminate, nor abusers of themselves with mankind, Nor thieves, nor covetous, nor drunkards, nor revilers, nor extortioners, shall inherit the kingdom of God. And such were some of you: but ye are washed, but ye are sanctified, but ye are justified in the name of the Lord Jesus, and by the Spirit of our God (I Cor. 9–11).*
>
> *Forasmuch as ye know that ye were not redeemed with corruptible things, as silver and gold, from your vain conversation received by tradition from your fathers; But with the precious blood of Christ, as of a lamb without blemish and without spot (I Pet. 1:18-19.).*
>
> *But now in Christ Jesus ye who sometimes were far off are made nigh by the blood of Christ (Eph. 2:13).*

Numerous other passages could be cited, but these are sufficient to show "*all have sinned, and come short of the glory of God*" (Rom. 3:23).

The Divine mention of Rahab in the genealogy of Christ is evidence that she has important place in the study of types of the inspired word of God. "*And Salmon begat Booz of Rachab; and Booz begat Obed of Ruth; and Obed begat Jesse*" (Matt. 1:5). Therefore, she should not be denied proper consideration in one's study of the Scriptures.

Consider the following types seen in the life of Rahab.

Rahab: A Type of the Redeemed Church

1. Jericho was opposed to the people of God.
The world is opposed to the people of God.

2. Rahab was redeemed and became a bride (Josh. 2:1; Matt 1:5).
The church is redeemed and is the bride of Christ.

3. Salmon married his redeemed bride (Matt. 1:5).
Christ is married to His bride—the church (Rev. 21:2, 9, 17).

4. The king of Jericho wanted to destroy God's people (Josh. 2:3).
Satan wants to destroy God's people (I Pet. 5:8).

5. Rahab was offered—and accepted—a covenant that would save her (Josh. 2:1, 14).
The church is the group of people who were offered—and accepted—a covenant (the New Testament) that would save them (Jas 1:21).

6. The family of Rahab were the only ones promised salvation (Josh. 2:1; 6:7).
Members of the church are the only ones promised salvation (Gal. 3:26-27; Eph. 1:3; I Cor. 12:13).

7. The promise of salvation to Rahab was conditional (Josh. 2:19).
The promise of salvation to the church is conditional (Rom. 12:1-2; I John 1:7, 9 (note the word "*if*").

8. The household of Rahab had to remain in the house to be saved (Josh. 2:19).
We must remain inside the church (II Pet. 20–22).

All the Types and Shadows of the Old Testament

9. The house marked for salvation had a scarlet thread to differentiate it from other houses (Josh. 2:15, 18).

The scarlet blood of Christ marks His people for salvation (Rev. 1:5).

10. The sounding of the trumpets by the Jews who compassed the city of Jericho marked the day of that city's judgment (Josh. 6:4–20).

Judgment day is coming (Heb 9:27; I Cor. 15:24; Acts 17:30-31).

11. Those outside of Rahab's house were damned (Josh. 2:19; 6:25-26).

Those outside of the Lord's church will be damned (Matt. 7:21–23; Mark 16:16).

12. The saved were in but one house.

The saved are in but one church (Acts 2:47; Eph. 1:22-23).

The Judges:
Types of Christ

The book of Judges consist of twenty one chapters of apostasy and repentance. Each of the judges were appointed by the Lord with the exception of Abimelech, who was self-appointed over Israel. Abimelech was an evil man, who acquired his place as a judge over Israel by killing sixty-nine of his seventy brothers, all sons of Gideon, who had numerous wives.

> And Gideon had threescore and ten sons of his body begotten: for he had many wives. And his concubine that was in Shechem, she also bare him a son, whose name he called Abimelech (Jud. 8:30-31).

> And Abimelech the son of Jerubbaal [another name for Gideon] went to Shechem unto his mother's brethren, and communed with them, and with all the family of the house of his mother's father, saying, Speak, I pray you, in the ears of all the men of Shechem, Whether is better for you, either that all the sons of Jerubbaal, which are threescore and ten persons, reign over you, or that one reign over you? Remember also that I am your bone and your flesh.

> And his mother's brethren spake of him in the ears of all the men of Shechem all these words: and their hearts inclined to follow Abimelech; for they said, He is our brother. And they gave him

> *threescore and ten pieces of silver out of the house of Baalberith, wherewith Abimelech hired vain and light persons, which followed him.*
>
> *And he went unto his father's house at Ophrah, and slew his brethren the sons of Jerubbaal, being threescore and ten persons, upon one stone: notwithstanding yet Jotham the youngest son of Jerubbaal was left; for he hid himself. And all the men of Shechem gathered together, and all the house of Millo, and went, and made Abimelech king, by the plain of the pillar that was in Shechem* (Jud. 9:1–6).

One of the judges to rule Israel was a woman named Deborah, about whom we read in Judges four and five. "*And the children of Israel cried unto the Lord: for he had nine hundred chariots of iron; and twenty years he mightily oppressed the children of Israel. And Deborah, a prophetess, the wife of Lapidoth, she judged Israel at that time. And she dwelt under the palm tree of Deborah between Ramah and Bethel in mount Ephraim: and the children of Israel came up to her for judgment*" (Jud. 4:3–5).

Each of the judges, as noted earlier, was chosen by the Lord to deliver the people of God from destruction. Apostasy was common among the Lord's people during the time of these judges, just as apostasy is common among the Lord's people today. It is sad so many congregations of the Lord's people go a whoring after apostasy, and most often refuse to repent and seek to be restored to the Lord.

Each of the judges was called upon by the Lord, to deliver His people from a common enemy, even though each judge was faced with differing circumstances. The Lord's church today has a common enemy in Satan,

The Judges: Types of Christ

whose wiles are indeed troublesome for the Lord's people and His church. As children of God we must: *"Put on the whole armor of God, that ye may be able to stand against the wiles of the devil"* (Eph. 6:11).

When saints don the whole armor of God they can follow the *"captain of their salvation"* into any satanic battle which may arise. *"For it became him, for whom are all things, and by whom are all things, in bringing many sons unto glory, to make the captain of their salvation perfect through sufferings"* (Heb. 2:10).

Consider the following ways in which the judges served as a type of Christ.

1. Each judge (with the exception of Abimelech) was chosen by the Lord.

Christ was chosen by the Lord.

2. Each judge was faced with unique situations and always conquered their enemy

Christ helps His children to conquer their enemies regardless of the situation.

3. Each judge was able to restore the people to God.

Christ is able to restore His people to Himself and His Father.

All the Types and Shadows of the Old Testament

Ruth:
A Type of the Redeemed Church

Just as the Song of Solomon is an inspired love story, so is the book of Ruth. The book of Ruth is a story of love and redemption. Ruth represents the Church in several ways. Few consider the book of Ruth in their studies of Biblical types.

1. She left the her old life behind and began a new one (Ruth 1:16–18).

Christians leave their old lives behind and begin a new one (Rom. 6:1-7).

2. She owned a new husband as her master (Ruth 4:13–17).

Saints disown their former master and own Christ (Rom. 6:17-18).

3. She worked in Boaz's harvest fields (Ruth 2:1–3, 23).

Saints are to work in Christ's harvest (John 4:34-35; Matt 9:37-38).

4. She humbled herself before Boaz and cast her care upon him (Ruth 2:10).

The Church is to be humble before the Lord and cast her cares upon him (I Pet 5:6–7).

All the Types and Shadows of the Old Testament

5. She chose to be separated from her worldly family (Ruth 2:21–23; 3:10).

The Church is to be separated from the world (Rom. 6:1–4; II Cor 6:17–18).

6. She found rest in Boaz (Ruth 3:1–2).

The Church finds rest in Jesus Christ (Matt. 11:28–30).

7. She married her redeemer (Ruth 4:13).

The Church is married to Christ, her redeemer (Eph. 5:25–32; Rev. 19:7-9).

Boaz:
A Type of Christ

Boaz stands out as a man with a stalwart and sterling character in the Scripture. Boaz also serves a pristine portrait of Christ.

The account of Boaz and Ruth is a story of sincere love and devotion, not only to one another, but also to the Lord. The relationship between saints and the Lord should show the same kind of love and dedication. The Lord declared: *"If ye love me, keep my commandments"* (John 14:15). *"Ye are my friends, if ye do whatsoever I command you"* (John 15.14).

Both Boaz and Ruth are given space in the inspired record of the genealogy of the Lord. It does the Bible student best to favor learning the lessons of the Old Testament, wherein many portraits of New Testament are found. Paul, the apostle, was indeed correct, when he said, by inspiration: *"For whatsoever things were written aforetime were written for our learning, that we through patience and comfort of the scriptures might have hope"* (Rom. 15:4).

1. Boaz was from the tribe of Judah (Ruth 4:18–22; Matt. 1:1–5).
Jesus from the tribe of Judah (Rom. 1:3; Heb. 7:14).

2. Boaz was from the town of Bethlehem (Ruth 2:4).
Jesus from Bethlehem (Matt. 2:1–6).

All the Types and Shadows of the Old Testament

3. Boaz redeemed his bride (Ruth 4:1–12).
Jesus redeemed His bride (I Pet. 1:18; Rev. 5:9).

4. Boaz displayed constant acts of kindness (Ruth 2:1–18).
Jesus was involved in constant acts of kindness (John 20:30-31; 21:25).

5. Boaz kept the Law (Ruth 4:1–12).
Jesus kept the law (Heb. 5:8; Phil. 2:5–11).

6. Boaz was a provider of physical blessings (Ruth 2:15–23; 3:17).
Jesus is a provider of both physical and spiritual blessings (John 1:1-3; Eph. 1:3).

7. Boaz owned the field into which he sent his laborers (Ruth 2:1–18).
Jesus owns the field from which saints are labor (Matt. 9:25–38; Luke 10:2).

8. Boaz had to pay the price to redeem his bride, Ruth (Ruth 4:1–12).
Jesus paid the price to redeem His bride, the church (Acts 20:28; Col. 1:14; I Pet. 1:18-19).

9. Boaz was a mighty man (Ruth 2:1).
Jesus is Almighty (Matt. 28:18; John 3:35; 13:3).

10. Boaz was devoted to God (Ruth 2:4).
Jesus was devoted to God (John 9:4; 17:4).

11. Boaz was just (Ruth 4:1–12).
Jesus is just (Matt. 27:19; Acts 17:31; Rom. 2:16).

Boaz: A Type of Christ

12. Boaz Was Humble (Ruth 3:1–18).
Christ was humble (Phi. 2:5–11; Heb. 4:15).

13. Boaz offered Ruth physical protection (Ruth 2:9).
Jesus offers His children spiritual protection (Lk.12:32).

14. Ruth was to harvest only in the field of Boaz (Ruth 2:8).
Saints must harvest only in the Lord's field (Matt. 13:1–9, 18-30).

All the Types and Shadows of the Old Testament

Samuel:
A Type of Christ

Samuel is a well-known character of the Old Testament, mentioned in one hundred twenty one verses, including three verses of the New Testament.

Some history and facts about Samuel: Samuel was the last judge of Israel.

> "And they gathered together to Mizpeh, and drew water, and poured it out before the Lord, and fasted on that day, and said there, We have sinned against the Lord. And Samuel judged the children of Israel in Mizpeh. ... So the Philistines were subdued, and they came no more into the coast of Israel: and the hand of the Lord was against the Philistines all the days of Samuel. And the cities which the Philistines had taken from Israel were restored to Israel, from Ekron even unto Gath; and the coasts thereof did Israel deliver out of the hands of the Philistines. And there was peace between Israel and the Amorites. And Samuel judged Israel all the days of his life" (I Sam. 7:6, 13–15).

He was a prophet (also known as a seer) of God.

> "And all Israel from Dan even to Beersheba knew that Samuel was established to be a prophet of the Lord" (I Sam. 3:20).

> "All these which were chosen to be porters in the gates were two hundred and twelve. These

All the Types and Shadows of the Old Testament

> were reckoned by their genealogy in their villages, whom David and Samuel the seer did ordain in their set office" (I Chron. 9:22).

Samuel was also a priest.

> "Moses and Aaron among his priests, and Samuel among them that call upon his name; they called upon the Lord, and he answered them" (Psa. 99:6).

Samuel's birth was miraculous and announced by Eli, the judge and prophet who preceded Samuel. Eli informed Hannah that God would favorably answer her prayer for a son.

> Now there was a certain man of Ramathaimzophim, of mount Ephraim, and his name was Elkanah, the son of Jeroham, the son of Elihu, the son of Tohu, the son of Zuph, an Ephrathite: And he had two wives; the name of the one was Hannah, and the name of the other Peninnah: and Peninnah had children, but Hannah had no children.
>
> And this man went up out of his city yearly to worship and to sacrifice unto the Lord of hosts in Shiloh. And the two sons of Eli, Hophni and Phinehas, the priests of the Lord, were there. And when the time was that Elkanah offered, he gave to Peninnah his wife, and to all her sons and her daughters, portions: But unto Hannah he gave a worthy portion; for he loved Hannah: but the Lord had shut up her womb.
>
> And her adversary also provoked her sore, for to make her fret, because the Lord had shut up her womb. And as he did so year by year, when she went up to the house of the Lord, so she provoked her; therefore she wept, and did not eat.

Samuel: A Type of Christ

Then said Elkanah her husband to her, Hannah, why weepest thou? and why eatest thou not? and why is thy heart grieved? Am not I better to thee than ten sons? So Hannah rose up after they had eaten in Shiloh, and after they had drunk.

Now Eli the priest sat upon a seat by a post of the temple of the Lord. And she was in bitterness of soul, and prayed unto the Lord, and wept sore. And she vowed a vow, and said, O Lord of hosts, if thou wilt indeed look on the affliction of thine handmaid, and remember me, and not forget thine handmaid, but wilt give unto thine handmaid a man child, then I will give him unto the Lord all the days of his life, and there shall no razor come upon his head.

And it came to pass, as she continued praying before the Lord, that Eli marked her mouth. Now Hannah, she spake in her heart; only her lips moved, but her voice was not heard: therefore Eli thought she had been drunken. And Eli said unto her, How long wilt thou be drunken? Put away thy wine from thee.

And Hannah answered and said, No, my lord, I am a woman of a sorrowful spirit: I have drunk neither wine nor strong drink, but have poured out my soul before the LORD. Count not thine handmaid for a daughter of Belial: for out of the abundance of my complaint and grief have I spoken hitherto.

Then Eli answered and said, Go in peace: and the God of Israel grant thee thy petition that thou hast asked of him.

And she said, Let thine handmaid find grace in thy sight. So the woman went her way, and did eat, and her countenance was no more sad. And they

All the Types and Shadows of the Old Testament

> *rose up in the morning early, and worshiped before the Lord, and returned, and came to their house to Ramah: and Elkanah knew Hannah his wife; and the Lord remembered her. Wherefore it came to pass, when the time was come about after Hannah had conceived, that she bare a son, and called his name Samuel, saying, Because I have asked him of the Lord" (I Sam. 1:1–20).*

Samuel grew in stature, and was well favored by both God and man. Samuel had a godly mother and an extraordinary childhood. Samuel was also a teacher of men.

1. Samuel's birth was miraculous (I Sam. 1-2).

Jesus' birth was miraculous (Matt. 1:18-25).

2. Samuel spent time as a child in the house of God, the tabernacle (I Sam. 3:1-10).

Jesus spent time as a child in the house of God, the temple (Luke 2:42-49).

3. Samuel was a prophet of God (I Sam. 3:20; I Chron. 29:29; II Chron. 35:18; Acts 13:20).

Christ was a prophet of God (Deut. 18:15; Acts 3:22-23; 7:37).

4. Samuel was a priest of God (I Sam. 3:1; 10:8).

Christ is our High Priest (Heb. 3:1; 4:15; 5:5-6; 9:11,

5. Samuel was the last judge of Israel (I Sam. 7:3–17; Acts 13:20-21).

Christ is the last and supreme judge of all men (Acts 17:30-31; John 5:22–27; Acts 10:42).

Samuel: A Type of Christ

6. Samuel oversaw the transition of Israel into a kingdom (1 Sam. 10).

Jesus instituted the eternal kingdom (Col. 1:13; Matt. 16:16-18; Rev. 1:9).

7. Samuel spoke and was seen after his death (I Sam. 28:6-25).

Jesus spoke and was seen after His death (John 20-21; Luke 24; Matthew 28; Acts 1).

All the Types and Shadows of the Old Testament

David:
A Type of Christ

One can only imagine the number of sermons written and preached about King David. His name is recorded 1,139 times in the Scriptures. He was man considered by Inspiration to be of righteous character. We read in the Scriptures how David was a man after God's own heart. Consider:

> *"And Samuel said to Saul, Thou hast done foolishly: thou hast not kept the commandment of the Lord thy God, which he commanded thee: for now would the Lord have established thy kingdom upon Israel for ever. But now thy kingdom shall not continue: the Lord hath sought him a man after his own heart, and the Lord hath commanded him to be captain over his people, because thou hast not kept that which the Lord commanded thee"* (I Sam. 13:13-14).

Luke wrote:

> *"And after that he gave unto them judges about the space of four hundred and fifty years, until Samuel the prophet. And afterward they desired a king: and God gave unto them Saul the son of Cis [Kish], a man of the tribe of Benjamin, by the space of forty years. And when he had removed him, he raised up unto them David to be their king; to whom also he gave testimony, and said, I have found David the son of Jesse, a man after mine own heart, which shall fulfill all my will"* (Acts 13:20–22).

All the Types and Shadows of the Old Testament

Consider the number of ways in which David serves as a type of Christ.

1. David was chosen by God as the king of the Jews (I Sam. 16:7, 11-13).

Christ was chosen by God the be king (John 1:29-34, 49; 12:13–15, many additional passage can be cited).

2. David was ordained to be king by the Father (I Chron. 14:2).

Christ was ordained by the Father (Rom. 5:8-9).

3. David was sent by his Father (I Sam. 17:17-18).

Christ was sent by His Father (Rom 5:8-9; John 3:16; Gal. 4:4-6).

4. David faced a formidable foe, Goliath (I Sam. 17).

Christ faced a formidable foe; Satan (Matt. 4:1–11; Luke 4:1–13).

5. Rejected by his brethren (I Sam. 17:28).

Christ was rejected by his brethren John 1:11–13; 7:5

6. David was a shepherd (I Sam. 16:19; 17:15).

Christ is the good shepherd (John 10:1–21; I Pet. 5:4; Heb. 13:20).

7. David was a king who ruled over God's people (II Sam. 8:15; I Chron. 18:14).

Christ is the King who rules over God's people (Dan. 7:13-14; Zech.1:8; 6:12-13; Acts 2:33; Eph. 1:20–23; Phil. 2:9; Heb. 2:7).

David: A Type of Christ

8. David was anointed by the prophet Samuel to be king over Israel (I Samuel 16:13).

Christ was anointed by God (Luke 4:18; Acts 10:38).

9. David was anointed King on three different occasions!
- By Samuel (I Sam. 16:13).
- By the men of Judah (II Sam. 2:4).
- By all Israel (II Sam. 5:3).

Christ was anointed three times.
- By one called Mary who anointed His feet in the house of Simon the Pharisee (Luke 7:36-50).
- By Mary who anointed His head in the house of Simon the leper (Matt. 26:6–23).
- By the Holy Ghost (Acts 10:38; Heb. 1:9).

10. David suffered wrongfully (I Sam. 18:6–18).

Christ suffered wrongfully (Mark 14:25; Luke 23:4–15; 23:41–47; I Pet. 1:19).

11. David was born in Bethlehem (1 Sam. 16:1–4).

Christ was born in Bethlehem (Matt. 2:1–8).

12. David was a man after God's own heart (I Sam. 13:13-14; Acts 13:20–22).

Christ was a man of God's heart, being about His Father's business (Luke 2:49; John 4:34; Heb. 2:10).

13. David was a prophet (Acts 1:16; 2:29-30; Heb. 4:7).

Christ was a prophet (Matt. 24).

14. David began his reign as anointed king at age thirty (II Sam. 5:4).

Christ began His ministry at age thirty (Luke 3:23).

All the Types and Shadows of the Old Testament

15. King Saul tried to destroy David (I Sam. 18:6–18).
King Herod tried to destroy Christ (Matt. 2:13–18).

16. David's name means "beloved."
Jesus was the "Beloved Son" of God the Father (Matt. 3:17; 17:5).

17. David began life as a lowly individual (I Sam. 16:19).
Christ began life in a lowly state (Matt. 1:18–25; Luke 2:1–7; Phil. 2:5-8).

18. David was exalted to the office of King (I Sam. 16:13; II Sam. 12:7).
Christ was exalted to the office of King (Phil. 2:5–11).

19. The Holy Spirit came upon David (II Sam. 23:2; Acts 2:25–31; II Pet. 1:21).
The Holy Ghost came upon Christ (Matt. 3:13–17; Mark 1:10; John 1:31–34).

Ahithophel: A Type of Judas Iscariot

Ahithophel is not often considered when studying the types of the Old Testament, yet he serves as a type of Judas Iscariot. Jesus plainly stated concerning Judas, that Judas was the fruition of Ahithophel in type, saying: "*I speak not of you all: I know whom I have chosen: but that the scripture may be fulfilled, He that eateth bread with me hath lifted up his heel against me*" (John 13:18).

The betrayal of Ahithophel had serious consequences. Ahithophel was a counselor and trusted advisor to David. He betrayed David by conspiring with Absalom to overthrow him. The consequences of his betrayal were severe and led to the death of many soldiers, as well as Absalom himself. Ahithophel's character is comparable to that of Judas Iscariot. His betrayal of David was motivated by Ahithophel's anger toward David for his treatment of Bathsheba and Uriah.

After quoting a passage that initially spoke of Ahithophel, we are told:

> *When Jesus had thus said, he was troubled in spirit, and testified, and said, Verily, verily, I say unto you, that one of you shall betray me.*
>
> *Then the disciples looked one on another, doubting of whom he spake. Now there was leaning on Jesus' bosom one of his disciples, whom Jesus loved. Simon Peter therefore beckoned to him, that he should ask who it should be of whom he spake. He then lying on Jesus' breast saith*

All the Types and Shadows of the Old Testament

unto him, Lord, who is it?

Jesus answered, He it is, to whom I shall give a sop, when I have dipped it. And when he had dipped the sop, he gave it to Judas Iscariot, the son of Simon. And after the sop Satan entered into him. Then said Jesus unto him, That thou doest, do quickly (John 13:21–27.).

Consider the following ways in which Ahithophel was a type of Judas Iscariot.

1. Ahithophel was David's counsellor, a close associate with David (II Sam. 15:12).

Judas was Jesus' apostle, a close associate with Christ.

2. Ahithophel ate David's bread (Psa. 41:9).

Judas ate bread with Christ (John 13:21–30; Matt. 26:14–16, 20-25).

3. Ahithophel was called a friend of David (Psa. 41:9).

Judas called friend by Christ our king (Matt. 26:50).

4. Ahithophel conspired against David, the Lord's anointed (II Sam. 15:31; 17:21).

Judas conspired against Christ, the Lord's anointed (Matt. 26:14-16).

5. Ahithophel hanged himself (II Sam. 17:23).

Judas hanged himself (Matt. 27:3–5).

6. Ahithophel conspired with David's enemies (II Sam. 15:12–31).

Judas conspired with Christ's enemies (Matt. 26:14–16; John 18:1–3).

Solomon: A Type of Christ

King Solomon is best known for his wisdom, however, Solomon authored many songs and proverbs as well. Solomon serves as a type of Christ in numerous ways

> "And God gave Solomon wisdom and understanding exceeding much, and largeness of heart, even as the sand that is on the sea shore. And Solomon's wisdom excelled the wisdom of all the children of the east country, and all the wisdom of Egypt. For he was wiser than all men; than Ethan the Ezrahite, and Heman, and Chalcol, and Darda, the sons of Mahol: and his fame was in all nations round about. And he spake three thousand proverbs: and his songs were a thousand and five. And he spake of trees, from the cedar tree that is in Lebanon even unto the hyssop that springeth out of the wall: he spake also of beasts, and of fowl, and of creeping things, and of fishes. And there came of all people to hear the wisdom of Solomon, from all kings of the earth, which had heard of his wisdom" (I Kings 4:29–34).

> "And when the queen of Sheba heard of the fame of Solomon concerning the name of the Lord, she came to prove him with hard questions. And she came to Jerusalem with a very great train, with camels that bare spices, and very much gold, and precious stones: and when she was come to Solomon, she communed with him of all that was in her heart. And Solomon told her all her questions: there was not any thing hid from the king, which he told her not.

All the Types and Shadows of the Old Testament

And when the queen of Sheba had seen all Solomon's wisdom, and the house that he had built, and the meat of his table, and the sitting of his servants, and the attendance of his ministers, and their apparel, and his cupbearers, and his ascent by which he went up unto the house of the Lord; there was no more spirit in her. And she said to the king, It was a true report that I heard in mine own land of thy acts and of thy wisdom. Howbeit I believed not the words, until I came, and mine eyes had seen it: and, behold, the half was not told me: thy wisdom and prosperity exceedeth the fame which I heard. Happy are thy men, happy are these thy servants, which stand continually before thee, and that hear thy wisdom. Blessed be the Lord thy God, which delighted in thee, to set thee on the throne of Israel: because the Lord loved Israel for ever, therefore made he thee king, to do judgment and justice.

And she gave the king an hundred and twenty talents of gold, and of spices very great store, and precious stones: there came no more such abundance of spices as these which the queen of Sheba gave to king Solomon.

And the navy also of Hiram, that brought gold from Ophir, brought in from Ophir great plenty of almug trees, and precious stones. And the king made of the almug trees pillars for the house of the Lord, and for the king's house, harps also and psalteries for singers: there came no such almug trees, nor were seen unto this day. And king Solomon gave unto the queen of Sheba all her desire, whatsoever she asked, beside that which Solomon gave her of his royal bounty. So she turned and went to her own country, she and her servants" (I Kings 10:1–13).

Solomon: A Type of Christ

1. Solomon built a temple in which God was to dwell (I Kings 6; Acts 7:46-47).

Christ built the church in which the Lord dwells (I Cor. 3:16-17; Matt. 16:18; Acts 2:47).

2. Solomon was anointed as king (I Kings 1:33-34).

Christ was anointed as King (Luke 7:38; Matt. 26:6–23. Acts 10:38; Heb. 1:9).

3. God gave Solomon wisdom (I Kings 4:29–34).

Christ was filled with wisdom (Luke 2:39-40).

4. Solomon's reign was one of peace (I Kings 4:25).

Christ's reign is one of peace (Isa. 9:6; Luke 2:14; Acts 10:36; Rom. 5:1; II Cor. 5:19; Eph. 2:14–18; Col. 1:20–21).

5. Solomon was God's servant (I Kings 13:7-8).

Christ took on the form of a servant (Phil. 2:5-8; Matt. 20:26–28).

6. Solomon rode a donkey (I Kings 1:33).

Christ rode a donkey (Matt. 21:1-7).

7. Solomon was the son of David (II Sam. 12:24).

Christ was the Son of David (Matt. 1:1).

8. Solomon was a preacher (Ecc. 1:1).

Christ was a preacher (Matt. 4:23; 7:28-29).

All the Types and Shadows of the Old Testament

Elijah:
A Type of John The Baptizer

As others in the Old Testament have been given space on the walls of history, so Elijah has a Divinely painted portrait of his life and service to God, which serves as an ante-type, at which all should intently gaze upon and ponder.

Several passages of Inspiration mention Elijah. The historical record paints Elijah as a deeply important character, serving as an ante-type of John, the immersing one, in God's scheme of redemption.

The first Old Testament passage in which Elijah is mentioned begins in I Kings 17:1. He is introduced to us suddenly, prophesying that neither dew nor rain would occur for a period of three years because of the evils of King Ahab and the disobedience of the nation of Israel (cf. I Kings 16:33). Before this event we know nothing of the prophet. However, we find Elijah always busy doing the Lord's bidding.

Just as his life was filled with many victories for the cause of righteousness, the close of the life of Elijah was enveloped in great wonder:

> And it came to pass, when the Lord would take up Elijah into heaven by a whirlwind, that Elijah went with Elisha from Gilgal. And Elijah said unto Elisha, Tarry here, I pray thee; for the Lord hath sent me to Bethel.
>
> And Elisha said unto him, As the Lord liveth, and as thy soul liveth, I will not leave thee. So they

went down to Bethel.

And the sons of the prophets that were at Bethel came forth to Elisha, and said unto him, Knowest thou that the Lord will take away thy master from thy head to day?

And he said, Yea, I know it; hold ye your peace.

And Elijah said unto him, Elisha, tarry here, I pray thee; for the Lord hath sent me to Jericho.

And he said, As the Lord liveth, and as thy soul liveth, I will not leave thee. So they came to Jericho.

And the sons of the prophets that were at Jericho came to Elisha, and said unto him, Knowest thou that the Lord will take away thy master from thy head to day?

And he answered, Yea, I know it; hold ye your peace.

And Elijah said unto him, Tarry, I pray thee, here; for the Lord hath sent me to Jordan.

And he said, As the Lord liveth, and as thy soul liveth, I will not leave thee. And they two went on. And fifty men of the sons of the prophets went, and stood to view afar off: and they two stood by Jordan.

And Elijah took his mantle, and wrapped it together, and smote the waters, and they were divided hither and thither, so that they two went over on dry ground. And it came to pass, when they were gone over, that Elijah said unto Elisha, Ask what I shall do for thee, before I be taken away from thee.

And Elisha said, I pray thee, let a double portion of thy spirit be upon me.

Elijah: A Type of John the Baptizer

And he said, Thou hast asked a hard thing: nevertheless, if thou see me when I am taken from thee, it shall be so unto thee; but if not, it shall not be so.

And it came to pass, as they still went on, and talked, that, behold, there appeared a chariot of fire, and horses of fire, and parted them both asunder; and Elijah went up by a whirlwind into heaven. And Elisha saw it, and he cried, My father, my father, the chariot of Israel, and the horsemen thereof.

And he saw him no more: and he took hold of his own clothes, and rent them in two pieces. He took up also the mantle of Elijah that fell from him, and went back, and stood by the bank of Jordan; And he took the mantle of Elijah that fell from him, and smote the waters, and said, Where is the Lord God of Elijah? and when he also had smitten the waters, they parted hither and thither: and Elisha went over (II Kings 2:1–14).

Elijah was present during the transfiguration of Jesus, appearing with Moses and Christ in glory. While Matthew and Mark tell us Moses and Elijah appeared with Christ, Luke tells us both were also transfigured in glorified form. This teaches us departed saints receive a glorious state. Paul tells us: "*For our conversation is in heaven; from whence also we look for the Savior, the Lord Jesus Christ: Who shall change our vile body, that it may be fashioned like unto his glorious body, according to the working whereby he is able even to subdue all things unto himself*" (Phil. 3:20-21). Further, we learn from the inspired hand of John, who wrote: "*Beloved, now are we the sons of God, and it doth not yet appear what we shall be: but we know that, when he shall appear, we shall be like him; for we shall see him as he is*" (I John 3:2).

All the Types and Shadows of the Old Testament

Mark's account tells us:

> *And after six days Jesus taketh with him Peter, and James, and John, and leadeth them up into an high mountain apart by themselves: and he was transfigured before them. And his raiment became shining, exceeding white as snow; so as no fuller on earth can white them. And there appeared unto them Elias with Moses: and they were talking with Jesus.*
>
> *And Peter answered and said to Jesus, Master, it is good for us to be here: and let us make three tabernacles; one for thee, and one for Moses, and one for Elias. For he wist not what to say; for they were sore afraid.*
>
> *And there was a cloud that overshadowed them: and a voice came out of the cloud, saying, This is my beloved Son: hear him. And suddenly, when they had looked round about, they saw no man any more, save Jesus only with themselves.*
>
> *And as they came down from the mountain, he charged them that they should tell no man what things they had seen, till the Son of man were risen from the dead.*
>
> *And they kept that saying with themselves, questioning one with another what the rising from the dead should mean. And they asked him, saying, Why say the scribes that Elias must first come?*
>
> *And he answered and told them, Elias verily cometh first, and restoreth all things; and how it is written of the Son of man, that he must suffer many things, and be set at nought. But I say unto you, That Elias is indeed come, and they have done unto him whatsoever they listed, as it is written of him (Mark 9:2–13).*

The Testimony of John the Baptist tells us he was the

Elijah: A Type of John the Baptizer

fruition of the ante-type of Elijah.

Matthew informs us that:

> "In those days came John the Baptist, preaching in the wilderness of Judea, And saying, Repent ye: for the kingdom of heaven is at hand. For this is he that was spoken of by the prophet Esaias, saying, The voice of one crying in the wilderness, Prepare ye the way of the Lord, make his paths straight. And the same John had his raiment of camel's hair, and a leathern girdle about his loins; and his meat was locusts and wild honey" (Matt. 3:1–4).

And John the apostle states:

> "And this is the record of John [the baptizer], when the Jews sent priests and Levites from Jerusalem to ask him, Who art thou? And he confessed, and denied not; but confessed, I am not the Christ.
>
> And they asked him, What then? Art thou Elias? And he saith, I am not. Art thou that prophet? And he answered, No.
>
> Then said they unto him, Who art thou? that we may give an answer to them that sent us. What sayest thou of thyself?
>
> He said, I am the voice of one crying in the wilderness, Make straight the way of the Lord, as said the prophet Esaias.
>
> And they which were sent were of the Pharisees. And they asked him, and said unto him, Why baptizest thou then, if thou be not that Christ, nor Elias, neither that prophet?
>
> John answered them, saying, I baptize with water: but there standeth one among you, whom ye

All the Types and Shadows of the Old Testament

> *know not; He it is, who coming after me is preferred before me, whose shoe's latchet I am not worthy to unloose. These things were done in Bethabara beyond Jordan, where John was baptizing" (John 1:19–28).*

We are told by the Lord that there was no one greater in the history of mankind than John. Even so, the faith of the greatest man waned on occasion. We must expect ours to do no less. However, we must overcome doubt and conquer of weaknesses.

> *"And it came to pass, when Jesus had made an end of commanding his twelve disciples, he departed thence to teach and to preach in their cities. Now when John had heard in the prison the works of Christ, he sent two of his disciples, And said unto him, Art thou he that should come, or do we look for another?*
>
> *Jesus answered and said unto them, Go and shew John again those things which ye do hear and see: The blind receive their sight, and the lame walk, the lepers are cleansed, and the deaf hear, the dead are raised up, and the poor have the gospel preached to them. And blessed is he, whosoever shall not be offended in me.*
>
> *And as they departed, Jesus began to say unto the multitudes concerning John, What went ye out into the wilderness to see? A reed shaken with the wind? But what went ye out for to see? A man clothed in soft raiment? behold, they that wear soft clothing are in kings' houses. But what went ye out for to see? A prophet? yea, I say unto you, and more than a prophet. For this is he, of whom it is written, Behold, I send my messenger before thy face, which shall prepare thy way before thee. Verily I say unto you, Among them that are born of women there hath not risen a greater than John*

Elijah: A Type of John the Baptizer

the Baptist: notwithstanding he that is least in the kingdom of heaven is greater than he. And from the days of John the Baptist until now the kingdom of heaven suffereth violence, and the violent take it by force. For all the prophets and the law prophesied until John. And if ye will receive it, this is Elias, which was for to come. He that hath ears to hear, let him hear (Matt. 11:1–13).

Comparisons which show Elijah to be an anti-type of John the baptizer.

1. Elijah preached the message of repentance (I Kings 18:20–40).

John preached the message of repentance (Matt. 3:1–2).

2. Elijah wore raiment of camel's hair (II Kings 1:7–8).

John wore raiment of camel's hair (Matt. 3:4).

3. Elijah preached against the evil king Ahab (I Kings 18:1–19).

John preached against the evil king Herod (Matt. 14:1–4; Mark 6:14–18).

4. A wicked queen sought to kill Elijah (I Kings 19:1–4).

A wicked queen sought to kill John (Matt. 14:1–8).

5. Elijah became depressed (I Kings 19:4).

John became depressed (Matt. 11:1–3).

All the Types and Shadows of the Old Testament

Elisha:
A Type of Christ

Elisha's name means "God is salvation." He served as prophet of God about 150 years after David reigned over Israel. Elisha's ministry differed from that of Elijah's. Elijah's miracles focused on calling the Jews to repentance. Elisha's miracles were focused on solving difficulties for those with whom he came in contact.

Just before Elijah was taken to heaven, Elisha asked for a double portion of the Holy Spirit with which Elijah had been endowed. Even though Elijah said to Elisha: *"Thou hast asked a hard thing,"* it was done as Elisha requested.

> *And it came to pass, when the Lord would take up Elijah into heaven by a whirlwind, that Elijah went with Elisha from Gilgal. And Elijah said unto Elisha, Tarry here, I pray thee; for the Lord hath sent me to Bethel.*
>
> *And Elisha said unto him, As the Lord liveth, and as thy soul liveth, I will not leave thee. So they went down to Bethel.*
>
> *And the sons of the prophets that were at Bethel came forth to Elisha, and said unto him, Knowest thou that the Lord will take away thy master from thy head to day?*
>
> *And he said, Yea, I know it; hold ye your peace.*
>
> *And Elijah said unto him, Elisha, tarry here, I pray thee; for the Lord hath sent me to Jericho.*
>
> *And he said, As the Lord liveth, and as thy soul*

All the Types and Shadows of the Old Testament

liveth, I will not leave thee. So they came to Jericho.

And the sons of the prophets that were at Jericho came to Elisha, and said unto him, Knowest thou that the Lord will take away thy master from thy head to day?

And he answered, Yea, I know it; hold ye your peace.

And Elijah said unto him, Tarry, I pray thee, here; for the Lord hath sent me to Jordan.

And he said, As the Lord liveth, and as thy soul liveth, I will not leave thee. And they two went on. And fifty men of the sons of the prophets went, and stood to view afar off: and they two stood by Jordan.

And Elijah took his mantle, and wrapped it together, and smote the waters, and they were divided hither and thither, so that they two went over on dry ground. And it came to pass, when they were gone over, that Elijah said unto Elisha, Ask what I shall do for thee, before I be taken away from thee.

And Elisha said, I pray thee, let a double portion of thy spirit be upon me.

And he said, Thou hast asked a hard thing: nevertheless, if thou see me when I am taken from thee, it shall be so unto thee; but if not, it shall not be so.

And it came to pass, as they still went on, and talked, that, behold, there appeared a chariot of fire, and horses of fire, and parted them both asunder; and Elijah went up by a whirlwind into heaven. And Elisha saw it, and he cried, My father, my father, the chariot of Israel, and the horsemen

Elisha: A Type of Christ

thereof.

And he saw him no more: and he took hold of his own clothes, and rent them in two pieces. He took up also the mantle of Elijah that fell from him, and went back, and stood by the bank of Jordan; And he took the mantle of Elijah that fell from him, and smote the waters, and said, Where is the Lord God of Elijah? and when he also had smitten the waters, they parted hither and thither: and Elisha went over (II Kings 2:1–14).

Elisha did twice as many miracles as Elijah, thus he was indeed given a double portion of the Spirit with which Elijah had been given.

Miracles connected with Elijah:

1. Revives a widow's son (I Kings 17:17–24).
2. Prophesied judgment on King Ahab (I Kings 21:17–24).
3. Prophesied that judgment was diverted from Ahab to his son Ahaziah (I Kings 21:28–29).
4. Prophesied judgment on Jezebel (I Kings 21:20–24; II Kings 9:30–37).
5. Prophesied judgment on Jehoram (II Chro. 21:12-16).
6. Prayed for and prophesied the rain would cease, and bring drought (I Kings 17:1, 7).
7. Prophesied endless oil for the widow of Zarephath (I Kings 17:8–16).
8. Prayed for fire from heaven (I Kings 18:20–40).
9. Prayed for and prophesied rain from heaven for the first time in 3 ½ years, and ends the drought (I Kings 18:41–45).
10. Outruns Ahab's chariot (I Kings 18:46).
11. Calls down fire to consume a captain and his men (II Kings 1:10).
12. Calls down fire to consume a Second army captain and his men (II Kings 1:12).

All the Types and Shadows of the Old Testament

13. Divided the waters of the Jordan (II Kings 2:8)

Miracles connected with Elisha

1. Parted the Jordan with the mantle of Elijah (II Kings 2:14).
2. Purified water with salt (II Kings 2:19-21).
3. Cursed forty-two of the youths for their disrespect to God's prophet (II Kings 2:23-24).
4. Prophesied that a valley would be filled with water for animals drink (II Kings 3:16-17).
5. This water deceived the Moabites, who thought it was a valley of blood (II Kings 3:22).
6. Provided endless oil for a widow (II Kings 4:1-6).
7. Prophesied the Shunammite woman would have a son (II Kings 4:16).
8. Resurrection of the Shunammite's son from death (II Kings 4:34).
9. Removed death from a pot of stew (II Kings 4:40-41).
10. Increased bread to feed many (II Kings 4:43-44).
11. Cured Naaman of leprosy (II Kings 5:10-14).
12. Perception of Gehazi's transgression (II Kings 5:26).
13. Cursed Gehazi with leprosy (II Kings 5:26-27).
14. Caused an ax head to swim (II Kings 6:5-6).
15. Prophesied of the Syrian battle plans (II Kings 6:9).
16. Vision of the chariots and horses for Elisha's servant to have courage (II Kings 6:17).
17. Smote the Syrian army with blindness (II Kings 6:18).
18. Restore the sight of the Syrian army (II Kings 6:20).
19. The prophecy of the end of the great famine (II Kings 7:1).
20. The prophesied a nobleman would see, but not partake of the abundance (II Kings 7:2).

Elisha: A Type of Christ

21. Deceived the Syrians with the sound of chariots (II Kings 7:6-7).
22. Prophesied of the seven-year famine (II Kings 8:1).
23. Prophesied of Benhadad's death (II Kings 8:9-10).
24. Prophesied of Hazael's cruelty to Israel (II Kings 8:12).
25. Prophesied Jehu would smite the house of Ahab (II Kings 9:7).
26. Prophecy that Joash would smite the Syrians at Aphek (II Kings 13:14-17).
27. Prophecy that Joash would smite Syria thrice but not consume it (II Kings 13:18-19).

Comparisons between Elisha and Christ:

1. Elisha began his work at the Jordan River (II Kings 2:12-14).
Christ began His work at the Jordan River (Mark 1:9).

2. Elisha healed a leper (II Kings 5:10–15).
Christ healed lepers (Matt. 11:5; Luke 17:11–19).

3. Elisha resurrected the dead (II Kings 4:32–37).
Christ resurrected the dead (Luke 7:11–16).

- Christ is the resurrection (John 11:25).

4. Elisha fed a multitude (II Kings 4:42–44).
Christ fed multitudes (Matt. 14:15-21; 15:32–38).

5. Elisha had a covetous servant (II Kings 5:15–27).
Christ had a covetous servant, Judas (Matt. 26:14–16).

All the Types and Shadows of the Old Testament

6. Elisha pronounced judgment against his covetous servant (II Kings 5:15–27).

Christ pronounced judgment upon Judas (Matt. 26:21–25).

7. Elisha had a forerunner in Elijah (II Kings 2:1–14).

Christ had a forerunner in John (Isa. 40:1–3; Matt. 3:1–3; Mark 1:2–5; Luke 1:16-17, 75, 77; John 1:23).

8. Elisha received a double portion of the Holy Spirit (II Kings 2:9-14).

Christ had the Holy Spirit without measure (John 3:34).

9. Elisha acquired the followers Elijah (II Kings 2:15–25).

Christ acquired the followers of John (John 1:34–42).

10. Elisha foresaw coming judgments against Israel (II Kings 8:12).

Jesus foresaw coming judgments against Israel (Luke 19:41–44).

11. Elisha was betrayed by his servant Gehazi for profit (II Kings 5:20–24).

Christ was betrayed by His servant Judas for profit (Matt. 26:14-16).

12. Elisha had power over nature (II Kings 2:8).

Christ had power over nature (Matt. 8:23–27; Luke 8:22–25).

Hezakiah: A Type of Christ

Hezekiah was a great king for the nation of Israel. His name means *the might of Jehovah*.

He was king of Judah, the son of the apostate king Ahaz. Hezekiah ascended the throne at the age of 25 in the year B.C. 726. Hezekiah was one of the three most righteous kings of Judah (II Kings 18:5). His first act as king was to purge, repair and reopen the temple of the Lord. He offered splendid sacrifices with a perfect ceremony in the Temple. Further, he destroyed the brazen serpent, made by Moses (Num. 21:9), which the Jews made an object of adoration and worship.

When the kingdom of Israel fell, Hezekiah called the Jews to a Passover, which was continued for a period of fourteen days (II Chron. 29:30-31). Hezekiah made aggressive campaigns against the Philistines, and won many victories over them, which his father Ahaz had lost (II Chron. 28:18; II Kings 18:8). Hezekiah refused to bow to the king of Assyria (II Kings 18:7). War soon followed. Hezekiah "made a pool, and a conduit, and brought water into the city" (II Kings 20:20).

Hezekiah soon fell very ill and sent for the prophet Isaiah, who prophesied Hezekiah would soon die (II Kings 20:1). Hezekiah's prayer was heard favorably by the Lord. The Lord instructed Isaiah to and inform Hezekiah he would recover from his terminal illness and be granted fifteen years more to live (II Kings 20:2–6). An

All the Types and Shadows of the Old Testament

embassy coming from Babylon ostensibly to compliment Hezekiah on his convalescence, but really to form an alliance between the two powers, is favorably received by the king, who shows them the treasures which he had accumulated.

Isaiah asked Hezekiah "... What have they seen in thine house? And Hezekiah answered, All the things that are in mine house have they seen: there is nothing among my treasures that I have not shewed them" (II Kings 20:15; Isa. 39:4). For this foolish action of Hezekiah, Isaiah foretells the punishment that shall befall his house (II Kings 20:15).

There were two invasions which the army of Sennacherib, king of Assyria brought against Jerusalem. The first of these took place in the third year of Sennacherib, B.C. 702, and occupies but four verses in the inspired record (II Kings 18:13–16). Of the second invasion, there is a more detailed record (I Kings 18:17–19:37).

Sennacherib, king of Assyria, sent his army to war against Jerusalem, under two officers and his cupbearer, the orator Rabshakeh, with a blasphemous and insulting summons to surrender. But Isaiah assured the Hezekiah there was no reason to be fearful of the Assyrian army (II Kings 19:1–13). *"And it came to pass that night, that the angel of the Lord went out, and smote in the camp of the Assyrians an hundred fourscore and five thousand: and when they arose early in the morning, behold, they were all dead corpses"* (II Kings 19:35).

Hezekiah lived about one more year, and earned peace and glory. He slept with his fathers, after a reign of twenty-nine years in B.C. 697.

Consider the following ways in which Hezekiah serves

Hezekiah: A Type of Christ

as a type of Christ.

1. Hezekiah was a king over God's people (II Kings 18:1).

Christ is king over His people (Matt. 2:2; 27:11, 37; Mark 15:2, 9, 26; Luke 23:3, 37-38; John 18:33, 39; 19:19-21).

2. Hezekiah was a king who interceded on behalf of God's chosen people (II Kings 19:14–19).

Christ in the king who intercedes on behalf of God's chosen people today (John 17:9–19).

3. Hezekiah provided physical water for his people (II Kings 20:20).

Christ provides spiritual water for His people (John 4:1–14).

4. Hezekiah was healed from physical death (II Kings 20:1–11).

Christ can heal the spiritually dead (Eph. 2:1; Col. 2:13).

All the Types and Shadows of the Old Testament

Ezra: A Type of Christ

The importance of the book of Ezra is often overlooked by many Bible students, yet it stands as a great example of the many portraits found in the New Testament. The books of Ezra, Nehemiah, Haggai and Zechariah and are best considered together. These four were contemporary, thus their work warrants collective observation.

Ezra shows the reestablishment of the Levitical Priesthood and Ezra's efforts to build a new temple after the Jews returned from seventy years of Babylonian captivity.

Nehemiah covers the rebuilding of the walls and the city of Jerusalem which were destroyed by the Babylonian army. Like Ezra, Nehemiah received strong opposition.

> But it came to pass, that when Sanballat heard that we builded the wall, he was wroth, and took great indignation, and mocked the Jews. And he spake before his brethren and the army of Samaria, and said, What do these feeble Jews? will they fortify themselves? will they sacrifice? will they make an end in a day? will they revive the stones out of the heaps of the rubbish which are burned? Now Tobiah the Ammonite was by him, and he said, Even that which they build, if a fox go up, he shall even break down their stone wall (Neh. 4:1–3).

Haggai addresses the rebuilding of the temple which suffered cessation during Ezra's efforts. Just as Ezra

All the Types and Shadows of the Old Testament

and Nehemiah faced opposition, so likewise did the prophet Haggai. "*Thus speaketh the Lord of hosts, saying, This people say, The time is not come, the time that the Lord's house should be built*" (Hag. 1:2).

Through the prophet Haggai, the Lord said to the people who resigned form building the new temple:

> *Now therefore thus saith the Lord of hosts; Consider your ways. Ye have sown much, and bring in little; ye eat, but ye have not enough; ye drink, but ye are not filled with drink; ye clothe you, but there is none warm; and he that earneth wages earneth wages to put it into a bag with holes. Thus saith the Lord of hosts; Consider your ways. Go up to the mountain, and bring wood, and build the house; and I will take pleasure in it, and I will be glorified, saith the Lord. Ye looked for much, and, lo, it came to little; and when ye brought it home, I did blow upon it. Why? saith the Lord of hosts. Because of mine house that is waste, and ye run every man unto his own house. Therefore the heaven over you is stayed from dew, and the earth is stayed from her fruit. And I called for a drought upon the land, and upon the mountains, and upon the corn, and upon the new wine, and upon the oil, and upon that which the ground bringeth forth, and upon men, and upon cattle, and upon all the labour of the hands* (Hag. 1:5–11).

Zechariah tells of the need to return to the work of building a new temple and of a future temple the Messiah would Himself build.

Sixteen years after the Babylonian exile, construction of the new temple of the Lord had ceased. The Israelites let personal affairs push God's business aside. Haggai sternly scolded the people for building their own houses

Ezra: A Type of Christ

rather than the house of the Lord. Haggai insisted it was time to build a new temple for the Lord. Haggai also pleaded with the older Jews who had seen the former temple, built by Soloman, to remember how beautiful it was. The builders were motivated to work, and their faith was increased by Haggai's message.

In contrast to old Haggai, Zechariah was a younger prophet. Haggai used a stern tone in his preaching to motivate the Jews to return to building the new temple of the Lord. Zechariah, however, encouraged the Jews return to the task of building a new temple with a more mild message. Zechariah showed the Jews the importance of a new temple. Zechariah prophesied of a greater temple which Messiah would built in due time.

> Hear now, O Joshua the high priest, thou, and thy fellows that sit before thee: for they are men wondered at: for, behold, I will bring forth my servant the Branch...
>
> ...And speak unto him, saying, Thus speaketh the Lord of hosts, saying, Behold the man whose name is The Branch; and he shall grow up out of his place, and he shall build the temple of the Lord: Even he shall build the temple of the Lord; and he shall bear the glory, and shall sit and rule upon his throne; and he shall be a priest upon his throne: and the counsel of peace shall be between them both (Zech. 3 8; 6:12-13).

That new temple would be the New Testament church, established by Christ on the day of Pentecost, as recorded in Acts 2.

Jesus declared to the apostles He would build his church:

> When Jesus came into the coasts of Caesarea

All the Types and Shadows of the Old Testament

> *Philippi, he asked his disciples, saying, Whom do men say that I the Son of man am? And they said, Some say that thou art John the Baptist: some, Elias; and others, Jeremias, or one of the prophets. He saith unto them, But whom say ye that I am? And Simon Peter answered and said, Thou art the Christ, the Son of the living God. And Jesus answered and said unto him, Blessed art thou, Simon Barjona: for flesh and blood hath not revealed it unto thee, but my Father which is in heaven. And I say also unto thee, That thou art Peter, and upon this rock I will build my church; and the gates of hell shall not prevail against it. And I will give unto thee the keys of the kingdom of heaven: and whatsoever thou shalt bind on earth shall be bound in heaven: and whatsoever thou shalt loose on earth shall be loosed in heaven (Matt. 16:13–19).*

The three disasters which were the result of the destruction of Jerusalem (the destruction of the temple, the city, and the walls) needed to be corrected. The priesthood needed to restored in order for the Jews to properly worship the Lord. A new temple was necessary, and the city and the walls needed rebuilding.

Though Ezra made some progress in restoring the temple, he suffered strong opposition.

> *And when the seventh month was come, and the children of Israel were in the cities, the people gathered themselves together as one man to Jerusalem. Then stood up Jeshua the son of Jozadak, and his brethren the priests, and Zerubbabel the son of Shealtiel, and his brethren, and builded the altar of the God of Israel, to offer burnt offerings thereon, as it is written in the law of Moses the man of God. And they set the altar upon his bases; for fear was upon them because of the*

Ezra: A Type of Christ

people of those countries: and they offered burnt offerings thereon unto the Lord, even burnt offerings morning and evening (Ezra 3:1–3).

Now in the second year of their coming unto the house of God at Jerusalem, in the second month, began Zerubbabel the son of Shealtiel, and Jeshua the son of Jozadak, and the remnant of their brethren the priests and the Levites, and all they that were come out of the captivity unto Jerusalem; and appointed the Levites, from twenty years old and upward, to set forward the work of the house of the Lord.

Then stood Jeshua with his sons and his brethren, Kadmiel and his sons, the sons of Judah, together, to set forward the workmen in the house of God: the sons of Henadad, with their sons and their brethren the Levites.

And when the builders laid the foundation of the temple of the Lord, they set the priests in their apparel with trumpets, and the Levites the sons of Asaph with cymbals, to praise the Lord, after the ordinance of David king of Israel. And they sang together by course in praising and giving thanks unto the Lord; because he is good, for his mercy endureth for ever toward Israel. And all the people shouted with a great shout, when they praised the Lord, because the foundation of the house of the Lord was laid (Ezra 3:8–11).

Now when the adversaries of Judah and Benjamin heard that the children of the captivity builded the temple unto the Lord God of Israel; Then they came to Zerubbabel, and to the chief of the fathers, and said unto them, Let us build with you: for we seek your God, as ye do; and we do sacrifice unto him since the days of Esarhaddon king of Assur, which brought us up hither.

All the Types and Shadows of the Old Testament

> *But Zerubbabel, and Jeshua, and the rest of the chief of the fathers of Israel, said unto them, Ye have nothing to do with us to build an house unto our God; but we ourselves together will build unto the Lord God of Israel, as king Cyrus the king of Persia hath commanded us.*
>
> *Then the people of the land weakened the hands of the people of Judah, and troubled them in building, And hired counsellors against them, to frustrate their purpose, all the days of Cyrus king of Persia, even until the reign of Darius king of Persia. And in the reign of Ahasuerus, in the beginning of his reign, wrote they unto him an accusation against the inhabitants of Judah and Jerusalem (Ezra 4:1–6).*

Under the prophets Haggai and Zechariah the rebuilding of the temple began again.

> *Then the prophets, Haggai the prophet, and Zechariah the son of Iddo, prophesied unto the Jews that were in Judah and Jerusalem in the name of the God of Israel, even unto them. Then rose up Zerubbabel the son of Shealtiel, and Jeshua the son of Jozadak, and began to build the house of God which is at Jerusalem: and with them were the prophets of God helping them.*
>
> *At the same time came to them Tatnai, governor on this side the river, and Shetharboznai, and their companions, and said thus unto them, Who hath commanded you to build this house, and to make up this wall? Then said we unto them after this manner, What are the names of the men that make this building?*
>
> *But the eye of their God was upon the elders of the Jews, that they could not cause them to cease, till the matter came to Darius: and then they returned answer by letter concerning this matter*

Ezra: A Type of Christ

(Ezra 5:1–5).

The city of Jerusalem was laid in total waste and needed rebuilding as well as the gates of the city.

> *The words of Nehemiah the son of Hachaliah. And it came to pass in the month Chisleu, in the twentieth year, as I was in Shushan the palace, That Hanani, one of my brethren, came, he and certain men of Judah; and I asked them concerning the Jews that had escaped, which were left of the captivity, and concerning Jerusalem.*
>
> *And they said unto me, The remnant that are left of the captivity there in the province are in great affliction and reproach: the wall of Jerusalem also is broken down, and the gates thereof are burned with fire (Neh. 1:1–3).*

Consider the following crucial lessons which should be learned from these four books. First, the Lord's work will always face opposition. "*And as they spake unto the people, the priests, and the captain of the temple, and the Sadducees, came upon them, Being grieved that they taught the people, and preached through Jesus the resurrection from the dead. And they laid hands on them, and put them in hold unto the next day: for it was now eventide*" (Acts 4:1–3).

Second, those involved in the Lord's work will always face opposition. "*And after that many days were fulfilled, the Jews took counsel to kill him: But their laying await was known of Saul. And they watched the gates day and night to kill him. Then the disciples took him by night, and let him down by the wall in a basket*" (Acts 9:23–25).

Third, the Lord's work will always be accomplished. "*For my thoughts are not your thoughts, neither are your ways my ways, saith the Lord. For as the heavens are*

All the Types and Shadows of the Old Testament

higher than the earth, so are my ways higher than your ways, and my thoughts than your thoughts. For as the rain cometh down, and the snow from heaven, and returneth not thither, but watereth the earth, and maketh it bring forth and bud, that it may give seed to the sower, and bread to the eater: So shall my word be that goeth forth out of my mouth: it shall not return unto me void, but it shall accomplish that which I please, and it shall prosper in the thing whereto I sent it" (Isa. 55:8–11).

Ezra understood his first duty was to study the will of God, that he may have it in his own heart, before preaching it to others

That Ezra serves as type of Christ is seen in numerous ways; Consider:

1. Ezra was a priest of God (Ezra 7:11-12).

Christ is our high priest before God (Heb. 4:15).

2. Ezra was a scribe, or teacher of the law (Ezra 7:11-12).

Jesus was a teacher come from God (John 3:1-2).

3. Ezra was a rabbi, or doctor of the law, well learned in the Mosaic law, and in all that related to the civil and ecclesiastical customs of the Hebrew people.

Christ was a master teacher of the Mosaic law, and was the mediator of it (John 3:2; Gal. 3:19-20).

4. Ezra was a preacher (Neh. 8:5-8).

Jesus was a preacher (Matt. 9:35).

5. Ezra had the commission of the king (Ezra 7:1–6).

Christ had the commission of God, who is the everlasting King (Jer. 10:10; Luke 2:49; John 4:34).

Ezra: A Type of Christ

6. Ezra "*prepared his heart to seek the law of the Lord, and to do it, and to teach*" it (Ezra 7:10).

Christ both did and taught God's will (Acts 1:1).

7. The hand of the God was upon Ezra (Ezra 7:6, 9).

The hand of the Father was on Christ (John 3:2; Acts 2:22).

All the Types and Shadows of the Old Testament

Nehemiah: A Type of Christ

It is necessary to once again consider the importance of the books of Ezra, Nehemiah, Haggai and Zechariah together, since they were contemporary with each other.

The Book of Ezra shows the reestablishment of the Levitical Priesthood and Ezra's efforts to build a new temple after the Jews returned from seventy years of Babylonian captivity.

Ezra shows the reestablishment of the Levitical Priesthood and Ezra's efforts to build a new temple after the Jews returned from seventy years of Babylonian captivity.

Nehemiah covers the rebuilding of the walls and the city of Jerusalem which were destroyed by the Babylonian army. Like Ezra, Nehemiah received strong opposition.

Haggai addresses the rebuilding of the temple which suffered cessation during Ezra's efforts. Just as Ezra and Nehemiah faced opposition, so likewise did the prophet Haggai. *"Thus speaketh the Lord of hosts, saying, This people say, The time is not come, the time that the Lord's house should be built"* (Hag. 1:2).

Zechariah tells of the need to return to the work of building a new temple and of a future temple the Messiah would Himself build.

Observe the following concerning Nehemiah and his

All the Types and Shadows of the Old Testament

work:

1. Nehemiah mourned over Jerusalem (Neh. 1:4).
Jesus mourned over Jerusalem (Matt 23:37–29).

2. Nehemiah dwelt in a palace (Neh. 2:1).
Jesus dwelt in the palace of heaven (John 1:1–3; Phil. 2:6-9).

3. Nehemiah left his dwelling place (Neh. 2:5–6).
Jesus left his dwelling place (John 1:1–14; Phil. 2:6–9).

4. Nehemiah went to Jerusalem (Neh. 2:5–6).
Jesus went to Jerusalem (Luke 2:21–22; Matt. 20:17).

5. Nehemiah had relentless adversaries (Neh. 2:9; 4:1; 6:1).
Jesus had relentless adversaries (Matt. 4:23; Matt. 22:15-46; 23:1-34).

6. Nehemiah went to build Jerusalem to build the city and walls (Neh. 2:6).
Jesus went to Jerusalem to build His church (Matt. 16:18, Mark 9:1; Isa. 2:1-4).

7. Nehemiah preserved the names of the workers (Neh. 3:1-32).
Jesus preserves the name of His workers (Rev. 20:12).

8. Nehemiah set captive slaves free (Neh. 5:6–13).
Jesus sets captives of sin free (John 8:32; Luke 19:10).

9. Nehemiah was a made Governor (Neh. 5:14).
Jesus was made a king (John 1:49; Mark 15:2; Acts 2:33).

Nehemiah: A Type of Christ

10. Nehemiah suffered temptation (Neh. 6:1–14).
Jesus suffered temptation (Matt. 4:1–11; Heb. 4:14–15).

11. Nehemiah completed his task (Neh. 6:15).
Jesus completed His task (John 19:30; Heb. 10:10).

12. Nehemiah left his work in the hands of others (Neh. 7:1-2).
Jesus left His work in the hands of others (Luke 24:45–47; John 13:1–17:1; Acts 1:8).

13. Nehemiah returned to his palace (Neh. 7:1–2; 13:6–7)
Jesus returned to heaven, Mark 16:19; Luke 24:50–53; Acts 1:9–11).

14. Nehemiah restored the priesthood (Neh. 7:63–65; 10:28-39; 13:28-31).
Jesus established a new priesthood (I Pet. 2:9).

15. Foreign nations rejected by Nehemiah (Neh. 13:1–3).
Foreign nations accepted in Christ (Isa. 2:2–4; Acts 1:8; 10:45).

16. Nehemiah went back to Jerusalem (Neh. 13:6–7).
Jesus will return to take the saved to heaven (I Cor. 15:24; I Thes. 4:13–18).

17. Nehemiah rejected disobedient foreigners (Neh. 13:23–31).
Jesus accepts obedient foreigners (Eph. 5:23–32; Rev. 22:17).

All the Types and Shadows of the Old Testament

Zerubbabel: A Type of Christ

No little confusion surrounds Zerubbabel and Shesbazzar. Opinions are numerous, some hold to the notion Zerubbabel and Shesbazzar are one and the same. Zerubbabel is most often related to his Babylonian name based on the suffix bel. Bel was a god of the Babylonian empire and is generally considered to be the title of the supreme god among the Babylonians and the Canaanites.

The opinion to which we fetter ourselves is that Zerubbabel and Shesbazzar are two different individuals. The sixteen year lapse in the building of the Temple seems to lend credence to this opinion.

The name Zerubbabel means *out of Babylon*, sometimes identified as "the prince of the captivity." Zerubbabel is mentioned in the Scriptures numerous times. In the first year of Cyrus, king of Persia, Zerubbabel was living in Babylon, and was the recognized prince of Judah during that captivity.

Upon the issuing of Cyrus' decree to have the Temple rebuilt, Zerubbabel immediately began the work. He placed himself at the head of those of his countrymen whose spirit God had raised to go up to build the house of the Lord in Jerusalem. It is probable that he was in the service of the king of Babylon. Zerubbabel was appointed by the Persian king to the office of governor of Judea.

All the Types and Shadows of the Old Testament

After arriving in Jerusalem, Zerubbabel's work of rebuilding the Temple began immediately. In the second month of the second year of the return, the foundation was laid. The Samaritans, however, were successful in putting a stop to the work for the final seven years of the reign of Cyrus and through the first eight years of Cambyses and Smerdis. Zerubbabel appears to be blameless for this long delay. The suspension of work on the Temple lasted sixteen years. The Jews were busy building costly houses for themselves rather than building the Temple of the Lord.

After much opposition and many hindrances, the Temple was finally completed in the sixth year of Darius, and dedicated with great rejoicing. The other works of Zerubbabel are the restoration of the courses of priests and Levites and of the provision for their maintenance.

The exact parentage of Zerubbabel is somewhat obscure, from his being always called the son of Shealtiel (Ezra 3:2, 8; and 5:2). Zerubbabel is given Divine mention in the genealogies of Christ (Matt. 1:12; Luke 3:27).

Ways in which Zerubbabel serves as a type of Christ

1. Zerubbabel delivered God's people from the captivity of Babylon (Ezra 2).

Christ delivered us from the captivity of sin, death and the grave (John 8:36; 14:6 with 8:32; Rom. 3:24-25).

2. Zerubbabel built a new temple of the Lord (Ezra 3:8–13).

Christ built the church, the new temple pf the Lord (Zech. 6:12-13; Matt. 16:18).

Zerubbabel: A Type of Christ

3. Zerubbabel protected his people against the Samaritans who hindered the building (Ezra 4:1–12)

Christ protects His Church (John 10:1–21; Eph. 1:1–13; Phi. 4:1–20).

4. Zerubbabel was joined to God (Ezra 4:1–3; Hag. 2:4).

Christ is united to God (John 10:30, 38; 14:11; 17:20-21; Phil. 2:6; I John 5:7).

5. Zerubbabel is the signet in the hand of the Father (Hag. 2:23).

Christ is the seal of God (John 6:27; II Tim. 2:19).

All the Types and Shadows of the Old Testament

Types from the Book of Esther

The book of Esther is one in which the providence of God is clearly seen. Yet, the book nowhere records the name of God, nor does the book reference the Lord to even the slightest degree. Christ, the church, Satan, and God's chosen people are displayed in types in the book of Esther, but are not often considered, yet they are there for observant Bible students.

Ahasuerus was the King of Persia and Media and was also known as Xerxes, a name is found in Grecian history. Both King Ahasuerus and Queen Vashti made great feasts for their people. "*In the third year of his reign, he made a feast unto all his princes and his servants; the power of Persia and Media, the nobles and princes of the provinces being before him*" (Est. 1:3). "*Also Vashti the queen made a feast for the women in the royal house which belonged to king Ahasuerus*" (Est. 1:9).

The reading of the book of Esther is necessary to obtain the scope of these types. From this book the Bible student has four types pictured for consideration in the characters of Esther, Mordecai, Haman and God's chosen people (the Jews).

All the Types and Shadows of the Old Testament

Esther: A Type of Christ and the Church

1. Esther was willing to give her life on behalf of her people (Est. 4:16).

Christ perished for his people (Matt. 27:27–56).

2. Through Esther's willingness to die for others, God's enemies are defeated and God's people are given life and honor.

Through Christ's willingness to die, God's enemy (Satan) is defeated, and God's people (the church) is given eternal life and honor (John 15:13; I John 3:16).

3. Esther was vindicated and honored (Est. 2:16–18).

The church will be vindicated and honored by its king (Eph. 5:27; I Thes. 5:23; Rev. 2:10).

4. Esther was not in relationship with the King at one time (Est. 2:1–7).

Those in the church were not in relationship with the Eternal King at one time (Eph. 4:18; Col. 1:21).

5. She became the bride of the king (Est. 2:15–18).

The church is the bride of Christ its king (Rev. 21:2).

6. She made intercession on behalf of God's people (Est. 7:1–6).

Christ makes intercession for His people (Isa. 53:12; Rom. 8:27, 34; Heb. 7:25).

All the Types and Shadows of the Old Testament

Mordecai: A Type of Christ

1. Mordecai was a man of faith (Est. 4:13-14).
Christ was a man of faith (John 11:41-42; 4:34; 17:4).

2. Mordecai was persecuted without cause (Est. 5:9–14).
Christ was persecuted without a cause (John 15:25).

3. Mordecai was an encouragement to the king's bride (Est. 4:14).
Christ is an encouragement to His Bride (Rev. 2:10; 3:11).

3. Mordecai was given honor (Est. 6:1–13).
Christ was given glory and honor (Dan. 7:13-14; Phil. 2:6–8).

4. Mordecai was exalted (Est. 10:1–3).
Christ was exalted (Acts 2:33; Eph. 1:20–23; Col. 1:18; I Pet. 3:22).

All the Types and Shadows of the Old Testament

Haman: A Type of Satan

1. Haman hated the people of God (Est. 3:1–15; 9:24). Satan hates the people of God (I Pet. 5:8; Eph. 6:11; Jas. 4:7).

2. Haman was full of pride (Est. 5:9–14). Satan is full of pride (I Tim. 3:6; II Cor. 11:13–15).

3. Haman coveted praise (Est. 3:2). Satan covets praise (Matt. 4:9).

4. Haman coveted power (Est. 3:1–5). Satan covets power (Matt. 4:1–11).

5. Lost his battle to conquer God's people (Est. 7:7–10). Satan will lose his battle (Rev. 20:1-3, 10; Jude vs. 6).

All the Types and Shadows of the Old Testament

The Jews:
A Type of the Victorious Church.

1. Were promised victory (Est. 8:1–17).
Christians are promised victory (Rev. 2:10)

2. Prepared themselves for battle against their adversary (Est. 8:11).
Christians must prepare for battle against their adversary (Eph. 6:13–17; I Pet. 5:8-9)

3. The Jews destroyed their foes (Est. 9:1–19).
The foes of the Lord's church will be destroyed (II Thes. 1:5-9).

All the Types and Shadows of the Old Testament

Hosea:
A Type of Christ

The name Hosea means *salvation* and is a form of the names of Joshua and Jesus. Hosea was a faithful prophet and a type of Christ. His service as a prophet of God was during the time the Assyrian empire sought to broaden its borders. Israel went into Assyrian captivity in 722 BC. It seems as if his ministry ended prior to that event, not long after the death of Jeroboam II and the fall of Samaria.

> "*The word of the Lord that came to Hosea the son of Beeri, in the days of Uzziah, Jotham, Ahaz, and Hezekiah, kings of Judah, and in the days of Jeroboam the son of Joash, king of Israel*" (Hos.1:1).

Hosea's prophetic work began when the "*word of the Lord*" came to him. The kings of Israel continued in the sin of the *first* Jeroboam. The sins of Jeroboam made Israel sin (II Kings 14:24). These sins are recorded in I Kings 12. Jeroboam instituted the worship of golden calves, which he called "*gods...which brought you up out of the land of Egypt*" (12:28); he changed the place of worship from Jerusalem to Bethel and Dan (12:27-30); he appointed priests which were not from the tribe of Levi (12:31); he changed the time of the feast of tabernacles after his own heart, not according to God's mandates (12:32-33). Worshiping God according to one's wishes is called "*will worship*" (Col. 2:23).

God commanded Hosea to: "*Go yet, love a woman beloved of her friend, yet an adulteress, according to the*

All the Types and Shadows of the Old Testament

love of the Lord toward the children of Israel, who look to other gods, and love flagons of wine" (Hosea 3:1). The Lord subjected Hosea to a very difficult trial, for the purpose of showing His grace, love, and mercy for His people. All men have "*sinned and fall short of the glory of God,*" as Paul declared in Romans 3:23.

Hosea was instructed to love Gomer before he purchased and married her; even though she did not then love Hosea. God's love for His children is "*everlasting love*" (Jer. 31:3), but it is conditional. "*For when we were yet without strength, in due time Christ died for the ungodly. For scarcely for a righteous man will one die: yet peradventure for a good man some would even dare to die. But God commendeth his love toward us, in that, while we were yet sinners, Christ died for us*" (Rom. 5:6-8). Paul and Peter refer Hosea's relationship with Gomer, as recorded in Hosea 1:10 (Consider Rom. 9:25-26, and I Pet. 2:10).

Parallels between Hosea and Christ.

1. Hosea was instructed by God to take a woman of adultery to be his wife (Hos. 1:2).
Christ took a once-spiritually adulterous people for his bride (Eph. 5:25-33; Jas. 4:4).

2. Hosea paid the required price to redeem Gomer as his bride (Hos.3:2).
Christ paid the price to redeem His bride, the church (Heb. 9:22; I Pet. 1:18-19; Rev. 1:5)

3. Hosea made himself accessible to Gomer, so long as she turned away from her adultery and returned to Hosea (Hos. 3:3-5).
The love of Christ is available to those who turn away

Hosea: A Type of Christ

from their spiritual adultery (John 3:16; Luke 5:32; 13:1-5; 15:1-10; 17:3-4; 24:44-49).

4. Hosea wrote: *"out of Egypt I called My son"* (Hos. 11:1).

God sent an angel to call His Son, Jesus, out of Egypt (Matt. 2:14-21).

5. Hosea promised the Jews they would be saved by the Lord if they would repent (Hosea 1:7).

Christ saves obedient men today with the price of His blood (Acts 20:28; Heb. 9:12; I Pet. 1:18-19).

6. Those to whom Gomer was enslaved demanded a price (Hos.3:1-2).

The sins of men today demand the price of the Lord's blood and His death (Heb. 9:12; Rom. 6:23).

7. Gomer left her husband Hosea, and even then, he sought to have her back—but it required repentance.

Even when a church has left their first love and shut Christ out of their lives, Jesus still wants to have them back—but it requires repentance (Rev. 2:4-5; 3:19-20).

All the Types and Shadows of the Old Testament

Jonah: A Type of Christ.

Jonah lived during the reign of Jereboam II of Israel (ca. 793–753 B.C.). He was contemporary with the prophets Amos and Hosea, and shortly before Isaiah and Micah. Jonah was from Gath Hepher, a village of Zebulun four miles northeast from what would later be Nazareth (II Kings 14:25).

Jesus Himself makes it clear that Jonah served as a type for Christ.

> But he answered and said unto them, An evil and adulterous generation seeketh after a sign; and there shall no sign be given to it, but the sign of the prophet Jonas: For as Jonas was three days and three nights in the whale's belly; so shall the Son of man be three days and three nights in the heart of the earth.
>
> The men of Nineveh shall rise in judgment with this generation, and shall condemn it: because they repented at the preaching of Jonas; and, behold, a greater than Jonas is here (Matthew 12:39-41).

Consider eight ways in which Jonah serves as a type of Christ.

1. Jonah was sent by God (Jonah 1:1-2).

Jesus was sent by God (Gal. 4:4; John 10:36; I John 4:9-10, 14).

All the Types and Shadows of the Old Testament

2. Jonah was a prophet (II Kings 14:25)
Jesus was a prophet (Matthew 12:39–41).

3. Jonah was a preacher (Jonah 3:1–5).
Christ was a preacher (Luke 20:1).

4. Jonah slept on a ship during a storm (Jonah 1:5-6).
Christ slept on a ship during a storm (Matt. 8:23–27).

5. Jonah was awakened by those on board (Jonah 1:5-6).
Christ was awakened by the apostles on board (Matt. 8:23–27).

6. Jonah was in the belly of whale for three days and three nights (Jonah 1:17).
Christ was in the belly of the earth for three days and three nights (Matthew 12:39–41).

7. Jonah sacrificed himself for others (Jonah 1:7–16).
Jesus sacrificed Himself for others (John 10:15–17; Tit. 2:14; I Pet. 3:18).

8. Jonah Preached to the Gentiles (Jonah 3:1–5).
Jesus preached to Gentiles (Matt. 8:5–13).

www.ingramcontent.com/pod-product-compliance
Lightning Source LLC
Chambersburg PA
CBHW050242010526
44107CB00032B/1376/J